TELEVISION RESEARCH

Dedicated to Akiko, Brando, and Suki

TELEVISION RESEARCH

A DIRECTORY OF CONCEPTUAL CATEGORIES, TOPIC SUGGESTIONS AND SELECTED SOURCES

compiled by
Ronald L. Jacobson

McFarland & Company, Inc., Publishers
Jefferson, North Carolina, and London

ACKNOWLEDGMENTS: A book such as this one usually is not the work of a single individual. I have many people to thank, especially the scholars who think, research, write, and teach about television, the most popular and powerful of our mass media.

I also wish to express my gratitude to the following Fordham University students who assisted me in gathering information for this project: Paul Alfarone, Edith Bellinghausen, Daniel Bergin, Nicole Boucher, Meghan Bradley, Gisela Burgos, Brendan Burke, Timothy Burke, Arlene Caban, Allison Cain, Cynthia Canzano, Jennifer Chandler, Elias Chios, Scott Chiovaro, Teresa Cicala, Dana Cilento, Kerri Cmar, Catherine Cryan, Charlie Cucchiara, James Deneen, Ann Dolan, John Dupuy, Marie Eliezer, Kenneth Feliu, Michael Friedman, Janna Gaffney, Jean Gildea, Christian Gonzalez, Jennifer Griesbach, Madeline Hernandez, Teresa Hillerman, Scott Horton, Craig Iovino, Jason Jacobs, Christopher Jones, Philip Kaso, Jane Kearney, Andreas Keller, Colleen Kiely, Edward Kiley, Lori La Salvia, Carolina Laise, Victoria Mallon, Christine Mangieri, Anna Marnikovic, Ed Martinez, Karen Mercado, Peggy Messina, Linda Miranda, Ingrid Molano, Barbara Moran, Denice Murray, Patrick Nolan, Walter Novak, Tara O'Brien, Vanessa Osso, Maria Panos, Roslyn Payne, Adelina Porco, Jennifer Pulick, Richard Quon, Maria Rizzo, Bryan Robinson, Jacqueline Salazar, Luis Salgado-Clara, Yesenia Santiago, Andrew Sherriff, Darach Smith, Joseph Stajek, John Sullivan, Christine Tauhert, Cesar Taveras, Marc Tessitore, Warren Tom, Lori Valvano, Marc Votto, Joseph Vuolo, Bevin Wands, Brian Weick, and Leighton Wynter.

The Duane Library at Fordham University in the Bronx, the New York City Public Library, and the Greenwich, Connecticut Public Library were essential in doing this project.

British Library Cataloguing-in-Publication data are available

Library of Congress Cataloguing-in-Publication data available

Jacobson, Ronald L., 1956–
    Television research : a directory of conceptual categories, topic
suggestions and selected sources / compiled by Ronald L. Jacobson.
      p. cm.
    Includes bibliographical references and index.
    ISBN 0-7864-0033-1 (softcover: 55# alk. paper) ∞
    1. Television broadcasting—Research—United States.
    2. Television broadcasting—Research—United States—Bibliography.
I. Title.
PN1992.3.U5J23   1995
016.79145'0973 — dc20
                                          94-44118
                                              CIP

Manufactured in the United States of America

McFarland & Company, Inc., Publishers
Box 611, Jefferson, North Carolina 28640

TABLE
OF CONTENTS

CONCEPTUAL CATEGORIES

ADDITIONAL SOURCES

ABOUT
THE DIRECTORY

This directory consists of an alphabetical ordering of television-related categories. For each category, a brief conceptual overview is presented, followed by a list of relevant research or lecture topic suggestions and a bibliography of selected print sources (mostly books). Users should appreciate the directory as a reference tool intended solely as a guide to studying television and not as an end in itself. As such, the categories herein are not necessarily mutually exclusive; nor are the overviews, topic suggestions, and bibliographies meant to be comprehensive. Instead, this publication is intended to inform broadly, to stimulate critical thinking, and to serve as a catalyst for further inquiry.

An *Additional Sources* section is included at the end of the directory. General reference books, relevant indexes and databases, scholarly journals, popular magazines, newspapers, and trade publications are listed. Libraries and museums containing special television-related collections are also noted.

There always seems to be new print publications and electronic databases that provide access to television-related content. Please consider this directory as but one entry point to television research. Users are encouraged to solicit the expertise of a professional librarian in order to access the most relevant sources available on topics of interest.

CONCEPTUAL
CATEGORIES

ADVERTISING

Advertising is the dominant means of financial support and profit for most television stations and networks in the country. Essentially, the bottom-line purpose of most television programming in the United States is not to inform or entertain but to sell an audience to an advertiser. Today, because of the proliferation of programming on cable, direct broadcast satellite, and newer television technologies, advertisers can more narrowly target their preferred audiences. Companies and organizations purchase time on television, among other reasons, to introduce new products and services, maintain professional approval, enter new markets, boost sales, rise above the competition, and or combat unfavorable publicity. Political candidates use television advertising to inform, create positive images of themselves, or discredit their opponents. The principal goals of all television advertising are to attract viewers' attention and to promote a preference for something or someone.

In attempting to reach its goals, television commercials offer some of the best examples of state-of-the-art television production. Commercials often entertain as they inform, mostly through the use of fictional characters and settings. Embedded in the ubiquitous and repetitive commercial messages are appeals to various human motives, including affiliation, security, and sex. Stylistic approaches vary from the traditional problem/solution format to comparative product advertising to the more expressionistic music video-influenced "image message."

The average cost of making a commercial for network television is often more expensive on a cost-per-minute basis than making a network television program. In addition to high production costs, broadcast network television is the most expensive medium in terms of the actual costs of purchasing air time, with major events such as the Super Bowl selling for several hundreds of thousands of dollars per 30-second spot. Although expenses are high, television may be actually the most cost-effective and efficient medium for certain advertisers. Television

5

advertising allows major companies to reach millions of consumers simultaneously, often for just pennies per viewer (figured on a cost-per-thousand basis), which is less expensive than advertising in other media.

Television is the first U.S. mass medium that began as an advertising medium. (Newspapers, magazines, and radio were initially free of advertising.) When television began, it inherited from the radio industry the system of direct sponsorship of programs. Advertising agencies were among network television's first programmers, producing popular shows such as the *Texaco Star Theatre*. But by the late 1960s, advertisers had mostly disappeared from program production. Full sponsorship of individual programs gave way to *participating* advertising, whereby advertisers bought time in different programs, thus sharing sponsorship but losing much of their previous editorial control over program content.

Some scholars argue that corporate advertisers, who spend millions of dollars annually on television advertising, continue to wield significant power in structuring the parameters of television discourse. Critics also point to the omnipresent commercialism that has pervaded television, blurring the line between programming and advertising (e.g., product endorsements on game shows, product-inspired cartoons, the Home Shopping Network, and so on). Critics argue that, in the United States, social alternatives to the values of the television marketplace are disappearing. Despite such criticisms, an increasing number of the world's countries are allowing advertising as the means of financial support in privatizing or increasing their television service.

Television advertising in the United States is regulated by several governmental agencies, including the Federal Trade Commission (FTC), the Federal Communications Commission (FCC), and the Food and Drug Administration (FDA). Rules exist about making product claims, advertising during children's programs, and so on. In rare instances, Congress enters the regulatory arena, as it did in banning cigarette advertising in 1971. Also of importance are the television and advertising industries' self-regulatory policies, ways of policing themselves in an ongoing effort to avoid increased government regulation.

(See also Audience, Children, Industry, Politics)

Topic Suggestions

Advertisers' influence on television program content
Advertising agency and television network relations
Case history of how and why cigarette advertising was banned from television

Comparative advertising
Comparative analysis of television advertising in the United States with television advertising in one or more other countries
Critical analysis of a television advertising campaign
Critics' arguments against television advertising and the advertising industry's response
Economics of television commercial production
Gender stereotypes in advertising
History of the television advertising for a specific product or service (e.g., Merrill Lynch)
Impact of new media technologies (i.e., cable, direct broadcast satellite, interactive television, etc.) on broadcast television advertising
Influence of television advertising on children
Influence of television advertising on eating habits
Persuasive appeals in television advertising
Political campaign advertising in a local, state, or national election
Product placement in television programs
Relationship between television advertising and free speech protected under the First Amendment
Roles of the FCC and the FTC in regulating television advertising
Strategic considerations involved in the process of planning, producing, and buying time for television commercials

Sources

Andersen, Robin K. *Consumer Culture and TV Programming*. Boulder, CO: Westview Press, 1995.
Arlen, Michael. *Thirty Seconds*. New York: Farrar, Straus & Giroux, 1980.
Barnouw, Erik. *The Sponsor: Notes on a Modern Potentate*. New York: Oxford University Press, 1978.
Bartel, Diane. *Putting on Appearances: Gender and Advertising*. Philadelphia: Temple University Press, 1988.
Biocca, Frank, ed. *Television and Political Advertising*. Hillsdale, NJ: Lawrence Erlbaum Associates, 1991.
Diamond, Edwin and Stephen Bates. *The Spot: The Rise of Political Advertising on Television*. 3rd ed. Cambridge, MA: MIT Press, 1992.
Evans, Craig R. *Marketing Channels: Infomercials and the Future of Televised Marketing*. Englewood Cliffs, NJ: Prentice-Hall, 1994.
Ewen, Stuart. *Captains of Consciousness: Advertising and the Social Roots of the Consumer Culture*. New York: McGraw-Hill, 1976.
Fisher, Joseph C. *Advertising, Alcohol Consumption, and Abuse: A Worldwide Survey*. Westport, CT: Greenwood Press, 1993.
Goldman, Robert. *Reading Ads Socially*. London: Routledge, 1992.
Hall, Jim. *Mighty Minutes: An Illustrated History of Television's Best Commercials*. New York: Harmony, 1984.

Heighton, Elizabeth and Don R. Cunningham. *Advertising in the Broadcast Media.* Belmont, CA: Wadsworth, 1984.

Jhally, Sut. *The Codes of Advertising: Fetishism and the Political Economy of Meaning in The Consumer Society.* New York: Routledge, 1990.

Kaid, Lynda Lee and Kathleen J.M. Haynes. *Political Commercial Archive: A Catalog and Guide to the Collection.* Norman: University of Oklahoma, Political Communication Center, 1991.

Kern, Montague. *30-Second Politics: Political Advertising in the Eighties.* New York: Praeger, 1989.

McNeal, James U. *A Bibliography of Research and Writings on Marketing and Advertising to Children.* New York: Lexington Books, 1991.

Marchand, Roland. *Advertising the American Dream: Making Way for Modernity, 1920–1940.* Berkeley: University of California Press, 1985.

Poltrack, David. *Television Marketing: Network, Local and Cable.* New York: McGraw-Hill, 1983.

Price, Jonathan. *The Best Thing on TV: Commercials.* New York: Penguin, 1978.

Russell, Thomas and Ron Lane. *Kleppner's Advertising Procedures.* 11th ed. Englewood Cliffs, NJ: Prentice-Hall, 1990.

Rutherford, Paul. *The New Icons?: The Art of Television Advertising.* Toronto: University of Toronto Press, 1994.

Schihl, Robert J. *Television Commercial Processes and Procedures.* Boston: Focal Press, 1992.

Schudson, Michael. *Advertising, The Uneasy Persuasion: Its Dubious Impact on American Society.* New York: Basic, 1984.

Stewart, David. *Effective Television Advertising: A Study of 1000 Commercials.* Lexington, MA: Lexington Books, 1986.

Warner, Charles and Joseph Buchman. *Broadcast and Cable Selling.* Updated 2nd ed. Belmont, CA: Wadsworth, 1993.

Wernick, Andrew. *Promotional Culture: Advertising, Ideology and Symbolic Expression.* Newbury Park, CA: Sage, 1991.

White, Hooper. *How to Produce Effective TV Commercials.* 3rd ed. Lincolnwood, IL: NTC Publishing, 1994.

AUDIENCE

Television is popular and influential because so many people view it. Almost all U.S. households have at least one television set, and three-fourths of the population watch television every day. Over the last decade, the average household has had the television set in use for about seven hours per day, with the average person watching about 30 hours per week. Women watch more than men, the elderly watch the most, and teenagers watch the least.

Audience research in the United States is mostly quantitative; that is, the commercial industry is much more concerned with how and what kinds of people are watching than with what viewers think of programming and how it might influence their lives. Television ratings measure the size and composition of television audiences nationally and in over 200 local markets (geographic locations). The A. C. Nielsen Company is the principal television research organization in the United States, and their ratings reports influence both television advertising rates and television programming decisions. The bottom-line purpose of most television programming in the United States continues to be to sell an audience to an advertiser. Programs with high ratings can attract high advertising rates, so programs with consistently low ratings are usually canceled. In this system, some people believe the viewing public has considerable influence in shaping programming.

Advertisers spend billions of dollars annually for the right to try to capture viewers' attention and hopefully influence consumer behavior through commercials. Advertising agencies buy television time based on the program's *demographics*, a composite of viewers by such variables as age, sex, ethnicity, educational level, household income, and occupation; and *psychographics*, which concentrates on the "whys" of audience/consumer behavior, including values and lifestyles.

Qualitative audience research suggests that age, sex, educational level, and other demographic factors usually play a role in television program selection. A *uses and gratifications* research model suggests that

9

people also watch television for reasons such as cognition (to learn more about the world), diversion (relaxation), social utility (to have something in common to discuss with others), and withdrawal (escape). Other factors affecting television viewing selection include cost (e.g., "free" broadcast television vs. pay-per-view cable), availability, comprehension, and interest. Of the latter, researchers suggest that most audience members selectively attend to television messages that reinforce existing attitudes and beliefs.

For most of television's history, the three major broadcast networks (ABC, CBS, and NBC) have commanded the lion's share of the prime time audience, but that share began to erode in the 1970s and 1980s with the growth of cable and the emergence of VCRs. Cable allowed for a proliferation of channels that targeted specific demographic groups, leading to some fragmentation of broadcasting's mass audience. For example, MTV targeted young people, ESPN targeted sports enthusiasts, and the Lifetime Network targeted women. The future of television audiences suggests continuing fragmentation as well as more active viewers who will have greater choice and control over what they view and when they view (via VCR time-shifting, video rentals, video dial-tone and other interactive television technologies).

(See also Advertising, Minorities, Women)

Topic Suggestions

Advertising agencies and television audience research
Analysis of the audience for a particular television genre (e.g., religious programming)
Are minority viewers fairly represented by the A. C. Nielsen audience measurement system?
Are television audiences mostly active or passive?
Audience members' uses and gratifications of watching sports on television
Audience participation in television talk shows
Audience ratings and their influence on network programming strategies
Cable television and the fragmentation of the mass audience
The changing television audience in the United States
Comparative analysis of different methods for collecting data on television viewing (e.g., diary, aided recall, etc.)
Comparative analysis of the work of different television research companies (e.g., Arbitron, A. C. Nielsen, and AGB)
Comparative analysis of program selection and audience behavior in the United States and in one or more other countries
Demographic versus psychographic analysis of television audiences
Effects of age and gender on audience perceptions of television characters

Effects of television violence on young viewers
Effects of the VCR and multi-set households on television audience research
Family viewing habits (e.g., control over channel selection)
The future of audience measurement
The historical relationship between audience measurement during the "sweeps" periods and television advertising rates
Historical study of size of broadcast and cable television audiences
Historical survey of television audience research methods
History of the A. C. Nielsen Company
History of the technology used for conducting, analyzing, and reporting audience research
How television producers perceive their viewing audiences
How the "people meter" changed television audience research
Impact of new technologies on television viewing behavior
Influence of the remote control on viewers' channel selection behavior
Literature review of psychological effects of television on heavy viewers
The Media Ratings Council (formerly the Broadcast Ratings Council)
Oral histories of viewers who grew up without television
Profile of pay-per-view television audiences
Public television audiences
Quantitative versus qualitative television audience research
Repeat viewing of television series (reruns)
The remote control device and its influence on television viewing habits
The role of the viewing public in shaping television programming
Special television audiences (e.g., the hearing-impaired)
Television viewing behavior and school performance
Television viewing habits of the elderly
Unintended audiences: the effects of adult programs on child viewers
Uses and gratifications of television in penal institutions

Sources

Ang, Ien. *Desperately Seeking the Audience*. London: Routledge, 1991.
Ball-Rokeach, Sandra J. and Muriel G. Cantor, eds. *Media, Audience and Social Structure*. London: Sage, 1986.
Barwise, Patrick and Andrew Ehrenberg. *TV and Its Audience*. London: Sage, 1989.
Berman, Ronald. *How Television Sees Its Audience*. Beverly Hills, CA: Sage, 1987.
Beville, Hugh Malcolm, Jr., *Audience Ratings: Radio, Television, Cable*. Rev. ed. Hillsdale, NJ: Lawrence Erlbaum Associates, 1988.
Bower, Robert T. *The Changing Television Audience in America*. New York: Columbia University Press, 1985.
Broadcast Rating Council. *Understanding Broadcast Ratings*. New York: BRC, 1978.

Buzzard, Karen. *Chains of Gold: Marketing the Ratings and Rating the Markets*. Metuchen, NJ: Scarecrow Press, 1990.

Buzzard, Karen. *Electronic Media Ratings: Turning Audiences into Dollars and Sense*. Boston: Focal Press, 1992.

Cantor, Muriel G. *The Hollywood TV Producer: His Work and His Audience*. New York: Transaction Publishers, 1987.

Cantor, Muriel G and Joel M. Cantor. *Prime-Time Television: Content and Control*. 2nd ed. Newbury Park, CA: Sage, 1992.

Day-Lewis, Sean, ed. *One Day in the Life of Television*. London: Grafton Books, 1989.

Drummond, Phillip and Richard Paterson, eds. *Television and its Audience: International Research Perspectives*. Bloomington: Indiana University Press, 1988.

Frank, Ronald E. and Marshall G. Greenberg. *Audiences for Public Television*. Beverly Hills, CA: Sage, 1982.

Frank, Ronald E. and Marshall G. Greenberg. *The Public's Use of Television: Who Watches and Why*. Beverly Hills, CA: Sage, 1980.

Fuller, Linda K. *The Cosby Show: Audiences, Impact, and Implications*. Westport, CT: Greenwood Press, 1992.

Hartshorn, G. G. *Audience Research Sourcebook*. Washington, D.C.: National Association of Broadcasters.

Huston, Aletha C., et al. *Big World, Small Screen: The Role of Television in American Society*. Lincoln: University of Nebraska Press, 1992.

Jenkins, Henry. *Textual Poachers: TV Fans and Participatory Culture*. New York: Routledge, 1992.

Kubey, Robert and Mihaly Csikszentmihalyi. *Television and the Quality of Life: How Viewing Shapes Everyday Experience*. Hillsdale, NJ: Lawrence Erlbaum Associates, 1990.

Levy, Mark and B. Gunter. *Home Video and the Changing Nature of The TV Audience*. London: John Libbey, 1988.

Lewis, Justin. *The Ideological Octopus: An Exploration of Television and its Audience*. New York: Routledge, 1991.

Lewis, Lisa, ed. *The Adoring Audience: Fan Culture and Popular Media*. London: Routledge, 1992.

Livingstone, Sonia. *Making Sense of Television: The Psychology of Audience Interpretation*. New York: Pergamon Books, 1990.

Livingstone, Sonia and Peter Lunt. *Talk on Television: Audience Participation and Public Debate*. London: Routledge, 1993.

Lull, James. *Inside Family Viewing: Ethnographic Research on Television's Audiences*. London: Routledge, 1990.

Morley, David. *TV Audiences and Cultural Studies*. London: Routledge, 1992.

Muller, Werner and Manfred Meyer, compilers. *Children and Families Watching Television: A Bibliography of Research on Viewing Processes*. Munich and New York: K.G. Saur, 1985.

Nielsen Media Research. *Nielsen Report on Television*. Northbrook, IL: Nielsen Media Research. Annual.

Neuman, W. Russell. *The Future of the Mass Audience*. New York: Cambridge University Press, 1991.

Seiter, Ellen, "Making Distinctions in TV Audience Research: Case Study of a Troubling Interview," in *Television: The Critical View*. 5th ed. Edited by Horace Newcomb. New York: Oxford University Press, 1994.

Seiter, Ellen, Hans Borchers, Gabriele Kreutzner, and Eva-Maria Warth, eds. *Remote Control: Television, Audiences, and Cultural Power*. London: Routledge, 1989.

Selnow, Gary W. and Richard R. Gilbert. *Society's Impact on Television: How the Viewing Public Shapes Television Programming*. Westport, CT: Praeger, 1993.

Spigel, L. and D. Mann, eds. *Private Screenings: Television and the Female Consumer*. Minneapolis, MN: University of Minnesota Press, 1992.

Steiner, Gary. *The People Look at Television: A Study of Audience Attitudes*. New York: Knopf, 1963.

Tulloch, John. *Television Drama: Agency, Audience and Myth*. London: Routledge, 1990.

Walker, James R. and Robert V. Bellamy, Jr., eds. *The Remote Control in the New Age of Television*. Westport, CT: Praeger, 1993.

Webster, James G. and Lawrence Lichty. *Ratings Analysis: Theory and Practice*. Hillsdale, NJ: Lawrence Erlbaum Associates, 1991.

BROADCAST STATIONS
AND NETWORKS

In the United States, broadcast television is essentially a local medium. Each station is licensed by the FCC to broadcast in the public interest to a specific market area on an assigned frequency on the VHF or UHF band. The larger markets, such as New York and Los Angeles, tend to have the most stations. Overall, there are approximately 1,470 television stations broadcasting in the country, with fewer than 20 percent noncommercial educational stations.

There are three basic types of commercial television stations. The first is the network owned-and-operated station. For example, New York stations WCBS, WNBC, and WABC are all owned by the networks reflected in their call letters. The second type is the network affiliated station, a station not owned by the network but having a contractual agreement with one to carry its programming. Over 60 percent of all television stations fall into this category. The third type is the independent station, which is not affiliated with a network and must secure all of its own programming.

Two other types of stations are worth mentioning. Superstations are broadcast stations beamed up to a satellite and made available to cable systems around the country. WTBS, Ted Turner's Atlanta-based independent UHF station, is recognized as the original superstation. Another type of station, the low-power television station, emerged with FCC approval in the 1980s with the hope of providing a greater diversity of programming to even more localized neighborhoods.

ABC, CBS, NBC, PBS, Fox—all are networks that do primarily two things; they sell advertising and provide programming to stations. "Network compensation" refers to the percentage of advertising revenue passed on from the network to its affiliates for carrying its programming. Networks produce their own programming, such as news, but the majority of programs are acquired for broadcast through licensing agreements with independent producers. In the 1990s, the FCC relaxed its rules so that the broadcast television networks can now produce and have greater financial ownership interest in more of their programming.

For approximately the first three decades of television, almost all viewers watched programming delivered solely by broadcast stations and networks. In fact, in 1976, over 90 percent of the prime time television audience tuned into stations carrying programs of one of the major three networks—ABC, NBC, and CBS. Since then, audience share has eroded by approximately 30 percent, due primarily to the popular growth of competing television technologies, particularly cable and the VCR. Today, broadcast stations and networks compete aggressively for viewers and advertising dollars. Group-owned stations and the networks also own and/or have financial interests in cable and other new television technologies.

(See also History, Industry)

Topic Suggestions

Analysis of ownership changes at ABC, NBC, and CBS in the 1980s
Case history of conflict between broadcast stations and cable systems: the must-carry rules
Comparative analysis of network versus local station advertising sales and revenue
Corporate history of a television network
David Sarnoff and William Paley: pioneers of network television
Economic analysis of network in-house production of news and/or sports programming
The FCC "freeze" on new broadcast television station licenses between 1948 and 1952
FCC regulation of broadcast stations
Financial interests of the television networks in broadcast-related businesses (e.g., owned and operated radio and television stations) and non-broadcast businesses (e.g., cable networks)
The future of broadcast television networks
Historical analysis of broadcast network share of prime time television audience
Historical analysis of relationship between networks and station affiliates
History of FCC regulation of network program ownership and syndication
How satellite technology influenced station and/or network operations
Licensees of public television stations in the United States
Low-power television stations (LPTV)
Non-English language television stations in the United States
Organizational structure and management of a major market television station

Organizational structure and management of a television network
Programming strategies of independent television stations
Publicity and promotion at a medium-market television station
The rise and fall of the Dumont Television Network
Rupert Murdoch and the emergence of the Fox Television Network
Technical analysis of FCC allocation of station frequencies on the electro-
    magnetic spectrum (e.g., VHF versus UHF allocations)
Television networks' response to pressure from public interest and special
    interest groups (on such issues as violent programming and depiction
    of minorities)
WTBS: the first of the "superstations"

Sources

Auletta, Ken. *Three Blind Mice: How the TV Networks Lost Their Way.*
    New York: Random House, 1991.
Bergreen, Laurence. *Look Now, Pay Later: The Rise of Network Broad-
    casting.* New York: Doubleday, 1980.
Block, A. *Outfoxed: Marvin Davis, Barry Diller, Rupert Murdoch, Joan
    Rivers and the Inside Story of America's Fourth Television Network.*
    New York: St. Martin's Press, 1990.
Boyer, Peter J. *Who Killed CBS?* New York: St. Martin's Press, 1988.
Broadcasting & Cable Yearbook. Washington DC: Broadcasting Publica-
    tions, Inc., annual.
Campbell, Robert. *The Golden Years of Broadcasting: A Celebration of the
    First 50 years of Radio and TV on NBC.* New York: Scribner, 1976.
Carter, Bill. *The Late Shift: Letterman, Leno, and the Network Battle for
    the Night.* New York: Hyperion, 1994.
Gitlin, Todd. *Inside Prime Time.* New York: Pantheon, 1983.
Goldenson, Leonard H. *Beating the Odds: The Untold Story Behind the
    Rise of ABC.* New York: Charles Scribner's Sons, 1991.
Hess, Gary. *An Historical Study of the DuMont Television Network.* New
    York: Arno, 1979.
Hilliard, Robert L. ed. *Television Station Operations and Management.*
    Boston: Focal Press, 1989.
International Television & Video Almanac. New York: Quigley Publishing,
    annual.
Krasnow, Ervin G. et al. *Buying or Building a Broadcast Station: Every-
    thing You Want — and Need — to Know, But Didn't Know Who to Ask.*
    2nd ed. Washington, DC: National Association of Broadcasters,
    1988.
MacDonald, J. Fred. *One Nation Under Television: The Rise and Decline
    of Network TV.* New York: Pantheon Books, 1990.
Metz, Robert. *CBS: Reflections in a Bloodshot Eye.* Chicago: Playboy
    Press, 1975.

Reel, Frank. *The Networks: How They Stole the Show*. New York: Charles Scribner's Sons, 1979.

Slater, Robert. *This. . . Is CBS: A Chronicle of 60 Years*. Englewood Cliffs, NJ: Prentice-Hall, 1988.

Sterling, Christopher H. and John M. Kittross. *Stay Tuned: A Concise History of American Broadcasting*. 2nd ed. Belmont, CA: Wadsworth, 1990.

Television Factbook: The Authoritative Reference for the Television, Cable & Electronics Industries. Washington, D.C.: Warren Publishing, annual.

Udelson, Joseph H. *The Great Television Race: A History of the American Television Industry 1925-1941*. Birmingham, AL: University of Alabama Press, 1982.

Williams, Huntington. *Beyond Control: ABC and the Fate of the Networks*. New York: Atheneum, 1989.

CABLE

Although cable television didn't become widespread until the 1970s, it actually began in the 1940s as community antenna television (CATV), a way of bringing television to mostly rural areas where broadcast signals were not reaching. Cable television has grown rapidly over the last few decades due to the development of satellite and microwave technologies which allow for the transmission of a wide variety of programming services. Today, well over one-half of all U.S. households pay a monthly fee for cable television to be delivered to them by cable companies that were originally given exclusive franchises to operate in particular localities.

Government regulation of the cable industry has been inconsistent, primarily because cable operates under a different set of guidelines than broadcasting, which uses the public air waves. For example, in 1984 Congress passed a law deregulating cable, and then, eight years later, re-regulated cable with another law. In addition to concern over cable companies' monopolistic pricing practices, the FCC has been concerned for years over the issue of whether cable systems should be required to carry local broadcast stations as part of their basic cable service. Early "must carry" rules were struck down as unconstitutional by the courts. Today, as a result of the complex 1992 law, local broadcasters even have the right to demand a carriage fee from cable operators. The battles between the broadcasters and cablecasters continue, while the telephone companies eagerly lobby for deregulation that will allow them to compete directly with cable by sending video via fiber optic "telephone line" wire to the home.

Narrowcasting on cable television allows programmers to target specific demographic and psychographic viewer-groups that are attractive to certain advertisers. Thus, there are cable networks devoted solely to movies, news, sports, music, home shopping, court trials, and so on. While basic cable subscription fees and advertising continue to be the main sources of income for the cable industry, pay cable services (e.g.,

HBO, Disney, and Playboy) and pay-per-view movies and special events also provide lucrative revenue.

U.S. cable systems, cable networks, and cable programs are owned and controlled by a relatively small number of large companies. The broadcast networks also have ownership interests in cable (e.g., ABC's ownership of ESPN). Public access to cable television is minimal. Municipally-controlled and public access channels are few in number, and those that do exist usually suffer from lack of funding and/or lack of public awareness and interest.

(See also Technology)

Topic Suggestions

Black Entertainment Television (BET): a case study of narrowcasting on cable television

Cable in the Classroom: a case study of an educational application of cable programming

The cable lobby: an analysis of the National Cable Television Association

Case history of cable in your particular geographical region

Comparative analysis of cable television and broadcast television programming strategies

Competition between direct broadcast satellite (DBS) and cable

Corporate analysis of a major cable television system operator (e.g., TCI, Cox, Cablevision)

C-SPAN: a public service of the cable industry

Economic analysis of cable home shopping networks

Economic analysis of pay-per-view cable

The future of the cable industry

Historical overview of cable regulation

History of public access cable television

Impact of cable television on local broadcast stations' audience ratings and advertising revenue

The influence of cable television on professional sports

John Malone: TCI's cable tycoon

The 1980s: a decade of consolidation and monopolistic practices in the cable industry

Ownership and control of cable networks and cable programming

QUBE: a case history of an early attempt at interactive cable

Significance of digital compression, enhanced sound, and other technological advances in cable technology

Telco (telephone companies) entry into television and the impact on the cable industry

Who watches cable: an analysis of audience demographics for basic and pay cable services

Sources

Bartlett, Eugene R. *Cable Television Technology & Operations: HDTV and NTSC Systems*. New York: McGraw-Hill, 1990.

Batra, Rajeev and Rashi Glazer. *Cable Television Advertising: In Search of the Right Formula*. Westport, CT: Quorum Books, 1989.

Broadcasting & Cable Yearbook. Washington DC: Broadcasting Publications, Inc., annual.

Brotman,, Stuart N. *Telephone Company and Cable Television Competition: Key Technical, Economic, Legal and Policy Issues*. Norwood, NJ: Artech House, 1990.

Chin, Felix. *Cable Television: A Comprehensive Bibliography*. New York: IFI/Plenum, 1978.

Dutton, William H., Jay G. Blumler and Kenneth L. Kraemer, eds. *Wired Cities: Shaping the Future of Communications*. Boston: G. K. Hall, 1987.

Engleman, Ralph. *The Origins of Public Access Cable Television, 1966–1972*. Columbia, SC: Association for Education in Journalism and Mass Communication, 1990.

Garay, Ronald. *Cable Television: A Reference Guide to Information*. Westport, CT: Greenwood Press, 1988.

Heeter, Carrie and Bradley S. Greenberg. *Cableviewing*. Norwood, NJ: Ablex, 1988.

Johnson, Leland and Michael Botein. *Cable Television: The Process of Franchising*. Santa Monica, CA: Rand Corporation, 1973.

Kenney, Brigitte L. *Cable for Information Delivery: A Guide for Librarians, Educators, and Cable Professionals*. White Plains, NY: Knowledge Industry Publications, 1984.

Nadel, Mark and Eli Noam, eds. *The Economics of Cable Television (CATV): An Anthology*. New York: Columbia University Press, 1983.

Negrine, Ralph, ed. *Cable Television and the Future of Broadcasting*. London: Croom Helm, 1985.

Philips, Mary Alice Mayer. *CATV: A History of Community Antenna Television*. Evanston, IL: Northwestern University Press, 1972.

Picard, Robert G., ed. *The Cable Networks Handbook*. Riverside, CA: Carpelan Publishing, 1993.

Sherman, Barry L. *Telecommunications Management: The Broadcast and Cable Industries*. New York: McGraw-Hill, 1987.

Television Factbook: The Authoritative Reference for the Television, Cable & Electronics Industries. Washington, D.C.: Warren Publishing, annual.

Yates, Robert K., et al. *Fiber Optics and CATV Business Strategy*. Norwood, MA: Artech House, 1990.

CHILDREN

Television plays a significant role in most children's lives. According to audience research, the average child in the United States watches 25 to 35 hours of television each week. By high school graduation, this average child will have spent more time in front of a television set than in a school classroom.

There are different needs and gratifications that cause children to attend to television as much as they do. One such need is to be part of a shared culture. Television programs, even though often viewed individually, are indeed "social events" that can be discussed with friends and schoolmates. Also, just as for adults, children turn to television as a pleasant diversion or as a form of escape from their own life-situations.

Concern over the time-consuming relationship between children and television has led to hundreds of research studies, public debate, and government regulation. Such concern stems not only from the popularity of the medium but from the realization that children make up a special audience. Children bring to the television viewing experience a more limited base of knowledge and cognitive skills than most adults. Nevertheless, children bring an eagerness to learn about the world from television. Unfortunately, they are only partially equipped with the necessary learning tools to successfully interpret, understand, and utilize much of the media content they are exposed to. Thus, polarized opinions abound about the value of television in the lives of children.

No one doubts the pervasive influence of television in many children's lives. However, it is difficult to generalize the effects of television because children are different. Each child brings a unique physiological, psychological, and sociological disposition to the viewing experience. It is also difficult to assess the influence of television because its effect on children is influenced by multiple variables including age, content, and the amount of viewing.

Age, by far, is the most determinant variable. For example, preschoolers tend to think some of what they see on television is real, a sort of "magic window reality." By age seven or eight, children begin to realize that even non-animated characters and stories may only be dramatic representations of segments of real life. As children get older, their critical thinking develops to a point where they can establish criteria by which to judge how realistic television content is.

Another significant variable affecting the influence of television on children is the content they tune to. Generally, research reveals that programs with the greatest influence, positive or negative, are those containing content that is familiar, repetitive, easily understood, realistic, and mildly arousing. Programs that encourage viewer participation or allow youngsters to identify with a principal character also tend to be effective. While some television content, such as *Sesame Street*, seem to exert a positive influence, it is other content, specifically advertising, violence and sex, that sparks most of the controversy concerning the relationship between children and television.

Age again is the most important factor in how children interact with television advertising. Research shows that young children often cannot distinguish the commercials from the program content. Seven to nine-year-olds usually can tell the difference. By age eleven or twelve, children realize a purpose of commercials is to persuade, not just to inform or entertain. Older children develop the cognitive ability to make choices based on an understanding of commercials' persuasive appeals and techniques.

Another area of concern centers on the nature of the causal relationship between televised violence and children's aggressive behavior in real life. Laboratory-type research studies show that not all children are affected similarly by televised violence. Generally, though, the short-term effect is that children with a disposition toward aggressive behavior will increase such behavior after viewing violent content. The research is not conclusive in terms of the seemingly more important long-term effects. Despite inconclusive research, several theories have been advanced about the effects of televised violence. A popular theory, called "observational learning," suggests children, who learn aggressive behavior in part by viewing it on television, come to perceive violence as an acceptable way to resolve conflict.

The issue of televised sex usually complements that of violence. As with televised violence, many of the programs with sexual content are intended for adults but also viewed by children. Children may not be mentally, physically, and/or emotionally ready to deal successfully with adult-oriented messages concerning aspects of mature interpersonal relationships. In terms of programming intended for children, the issue of sexual stereotyping has received considerable attention. Television is perceived by some scholars as an important source during the process by which children formulate both their sexual identity and their perceptions of gender differences.

(See also Criticism & Theory, Psychological Aspects, Regulation and Policy, Social Aspects)

Topic Suggestions

Case study of a public interest lobbying group: Action for Children's Television
Case study of Children's Television Workshop, producers of *Sesame Street*
Children and interactive television
Children, televised violence, and aggressive behavior
The Children's Television Act of 1990
Comparative analysis of children's television in the United States with that in one or more other countries
Comparative analysis of children's television programming on commercial broadcast television, cable television, and public television
Effects of television advertising on children
Ethnic representation and portrayal in children's television programming
Gender stereotypes and sex-role identification in children's television cartoon programming
Government policy and regulation of children's television
History of children's television programming
How children understand and learn from television
Impact of non-broadcast technologies (e.g., cable) on children's television
Kidvid: the children's video industry
Literature review of research on effects of television viewing on children
Parent-child interaction in the television viewing experience
Producing television programs for young children
Roles of networks, producers, and the public in determining children's television content
Uses and gratifications of child television viewers

Sources

Adler, Richard P. et al. *The Effects of Television Advertising on Children: Review and Recommendations.* Lexington, MA: Lexington Books, 1980.
Barcus, Francis Earle. *Images of Life on Children's Television: Sex Roles, Minorities, and Families.* New York: Praeger, 1983.

Berry, Gordon L. and Joy Keiko Asamen, eds. *Children & Television: Images in a Changing Sociocultural World.* Newbury Park, CA: Sage, 1993.

Bryant, Jennings and Daniel R. Anderson, eds. *Children's Understanding of Television: Research on Attention and Comprehension.* New York: Academic Press, 1983.

Comstock, George A. with H. Paik. *Television and the American Child.* San Diego: Academic Press, 1991.

Dorr, Aimee. *Television and Children: A Special Medium for a Special Audience.* Beverly Hills: Sage, 1986.

Feshbach, Seymour and Robert Singer. *Television and Aggression.* San Francisco: Jossey-Bass, 1971.

Fischer, Stuart. *Kids' TV: The First 25 Years.* New York: Facts on File, 1983.

Greenfield, Patricia Marks. *Mind and Media: The Effects of Television, Video Games, and Computers.* Cambridge, MA: Harvard University Press, 1984.

Gunter B. and Jill McAleer. *Children and Television: The One-Eyed Monster?* London: Routledge, 1990.

Gunter, B., Jill McAleer and Brian Clifford. *Children's Views About Television.* Aldershot, England: Avebury, 1991.

Hodge, Bob and David Tripp. *Children and TV: A Semiotic Approach.* Cambridge: Polity Press, 1986.

Kinder, Marsha. *Playing with Power in Movies, Television, and Video Games: From Muppet Babies to Teenage Mutant Ninja Turtles.* Berkeley: University of California Press, 1991.

Lesser, Gerald S. *Children and Television: Lessons from Sesame Street.* New York: Random House, 1987.

Liebert, Robert M. and Joyce Sprafkin. *The Early Window: Effects of TV on Children and Youth.* 3rd ed. New York: Pergamon, 1988.

Luke, Carmen. *Constructing the Child Viewer: A History of the American Discourse on Television and Children, 1950–1980.* Westport, CT: Praeger, 1990.

McNeal, James U. *A Bibliography of Research and Writings on Marketing and Advertising to Children.* New York: Lexington Books, 1991.

Muller, Werner and Manfred Meyer, compilers. *Children and Families Watching Television: A Bibliography of Research on Viewing Processes.* Munich and New York: K.G. Saur, 1985.

Palmer, Edward L. *Television and America's Children: A Crisis of Neglect.* New York: Oxford University Press, 1988.

Palmer, Edward and Aimee Dorr, eds. *Children and the Faces of Television: Teaching, Violence, Selling.* New York: Academic Press, 1980.

Palmer, Patricia. *The Lively Audience: A Study of Children Around the TV Set.* Sydney: Allen and Unwin, 1986.

Postman, Neil. *The Disappearance of Childhood.* New York: Dell, 1982.

Provenzo, Eugene F. Jr. *Video Kids: Making Sense of Nintendo.* Cambridge: Harvard University Press, 1991.

Schneider, Cy. *Children's TV: The Art, the Business, and How It Works*. Lincolnwood: NTC Books, 1989.

Schrag, Robert L. *Taming the Wild Tube: A Family's Guide to Television and Video*. Chapel Hill, NC: University of North Carolina Press, 1990.

Signorielli, Nancy. *A Sourcebook on Children and Television*. Westport, CT: Greenwood Press, 1991.

Simpson, Philip, ed. *Parents Talking TV*. London: Comedia, 1987.

Singer, Dorothy G., Jerome Singer and Diana Zuckerman. *Teaching Television: How to Use TV to Your Children's Advantage*. New York: Dial, 1981.

Singer, Jerome and Dorothy G. Singer. *Television, Imagination, and Aggression: A Study of Preschoolers' Play and Television Viewing Patterns*. Hillsdale, NJ: Lawrence Erlbaum Associates, 1980.

Turow, Joseph. *Entertainment, Education, and the Hard Sell: Three Decades of Network Children's Television*. New York: Praeger, 1981.

U.S. Surgeon General's Scientific Advisory Committee on Television and Social Behavior. *Television and Growing Up: The Impact of Televised Violence*. 6 vols. Washington, DC: U.S. Government Printing Office, 1972.

Van Evra, Judith. *Television and Child Development*. Hillsdale, NJ: Lawrence Erlbaum Associates, 1990.

Winick, Mariann and Charles Winick. *The Television Experience: What Children See*. Beverly Hills, CA: Sage, 1979.

Woolery, George W. *Children's Television: The First Thirty-Five Years, 1946–81. Part I: Animated Cartoon Series*. Metuchen, NJ: Scarecrow Press, 1983.

Woolery, George W. *Children's Television: The First Thirty-Five Years, 1946–81. Part II: Live, Film, and Tape Series*. Metuchen, NJ: Scarecrow Press, 1985.

Zillmann, Dolf, Jennings Bryant and Aletha Huston, eds. *Media, Children, and the Family*. Hillsdale, NJ: Lawrence Erlbaum Associates, 1993.

COMEDY

Most people like to laugh, which is one reason why humor on television, in advertising and programs, has been popular since the mass medium began. Television comedy found its roots in radio, and several of the early television comedians, including Jack Benny, and George Burns and Gracie Allen, originally starred in their own radio programs. Live television programs in the 1950s, such as *Your Show of Shows* and *Ernie Kovacs,* pointed to the potential of television as a medium for visual humor. Comedy on television has taken several forms, including physical slapstick humor and stand-up monologues. However, by far, the most popular form continues to be the 30-minute situation comedy.

The situational contexts of situation comedies have ranged from the ridiculous, such as *Mork and Mindy,* to the serious, such as *M*A*S*H.* Most situation comedies share a common structure in which a conflict arises but is resolved by the end of the episode. Over the last 40 years, situation comedies have evolved from relatively idealistic depictions of family life, such as *The Donna Reed Show,* toward more realistic portrayals, such as *Roseanne.* A major turning point in situation comedy came in the 1970s with Norman Lear–produced programs, particularly *All in the Family,* which commented on contemporary and sometimes controversial subjects. For example, *Maude,* a spin-off from *All in the Family,* featured a controversial episode on abortion, and dozens of CBS affiliates refused to broadcast the program. Today, fewer subjects seem taboo, as situation comedies comment on a wide variety of issues, including homosexuality and rape.

Comedy programming is on television during most parts of the day. First-run prime time comedies and late-night programs, such as *The Tonight Show* and *The Late Show,* are most popular, but syndicated reruns of past comedy hits are also popularly viewed during different times of the day. With the proliferation of cable networks in the 1980s and 1990s, more comedy than ever is now seen on television, including stand-up comedy from comedy nightclubs and comedy concerts. Comedy Central is a cable network dedicated entirely to comedy programming.

Television producers and syndicators export U.S. television comedy to other countries. The few comedies imported to the United States have been mostly British productions, such as *Benny Hill* and *Monty Python's Flying Circus*. However, some U.S. television programs, including *All in the Family* and *America's Funniest Home Videos,* have been adapted from similar programs in other countries.

(See also Programming)

Topic Suggestions

Audience uses and gratifications of viewing television comedy
Auteur analysis of significant comedy television producer (e.g., Norman Lear)
Biographical study of significant television comedian (e.g., Lucille Ball or
    Jackie Gleason)
Cartoons: examining the relationship between humor and violence
Children and television humor (including exposure to comedy intended for
    an adult audience)
Comedy Central (the all-comedy cable network)
Comedy programs: the transition from radio to television
Comparative analysis of British and American television comedy
Critical analysis of the evolution of types of humor and humor content in
    television comedy
Economic analysis of the syndication markets for television comedies
Evolution of the situation comedy
Exporting U.S. television comedies
Gender differences in television comedy preferences
Historical analysis of the depiction of families in situation comedies
History of HBO *Comic Relief* charitable event
History of *Saturday Night Live*
Humor in advertising
Laugh now: a critical history of the television laugh track
Live television comedy in the 1950s
Portrayals of minorities in comedies
Production analysis of a situation comedy
Role of comedy in late night television
Satire, political parody, and social commentary in television comedy
Sexual humor on television
Stand-up comedy on television
Stereotypes in situation comedies and their effects on social perceptions
Television humor and learning

Sources

Adler, Richard, ed. *All in the Family: A Critical Appraisal*. New York: Praeger, 1979.

Eisner, Joel and David Krinsky. *Television Comedy Series: An Episode Guide to 153 TV Sitcoms in Syndication*. Jefferson, NC: McFarland, 1984.

Grote, David. *The End of Comedy: The Sit-Com and the Comedic Tradition*. Hamden, CT: Shoe String Press, 1983.

Hamamoto, Darrell Y. *Nervous Laughter: Television Situation Comedy and Liberal Democratic Ideology*. New York: Praeger, 1989.

Henry III, William A. *The Great One: The Life and Legend of Jackie Gleason*. New York: Doubleday, 1992.

Jones, Gerard. *Honey, I'm Home! Sitcoms: Selling the American Dream*. New York: St. Martin's Press, 1993.

Kassel, Michael B. *America's Favorite Radio Station: WKRP in Cincinnati*. Bowling Green, OH: Bowling Green State University Popular Press, 1993.

Marc, David. *Comic Visions: TV Comedy and American Culture*. Boston: Unwin Hyman, 1989.

Marc, David. *Demographic Vistas: Television in American Culture*. Philadelphia: University of Pennsylvania Press, 1984.

Martin, Linda and Kerry Segrave. *Women in Comedy*. Secaucus, NJ: Citadel Press, 1986.

Mellencamp. Patricia. *High Anxiety: Catastrophe, Scandal, Age, and Comedy*. Bloomington: Indiana University Press, 1992.

Morella, Joe and Edward Z. Epstein. *Forever Lucy: The Life of Lucille Ball*. Secaucus, NJ: Lyle Stuart, 1986.

Neale, Steve and Frank Krutnik. *Popular Film and Television Comedy*. London: Routledge, 1990.

Nilsen, Don L. F. *Humor Scholarship: A Research Bibliography*. Westport, CT: Greenwood Publishing, 1993.

Rico, Diana. *Ernie Kovacs*. New York: Harcourt Brace Jovanovich, 1990.

Royce, Brenda S. *Hogan's Heroes: A Comprehensive Reference to the 1965–1971 Television Comedy Series, with Cast Biographies & an Episode Guide*. Jefferson, NC: McFarland, 1993.

Saks, Sol. *The Craft of Comedy Writing*. Cincinnati: Writer's Digest, 1985.

Sanders, Coyne S. and Tom Gilbert. *Desilu: The Story of Lucille Ball and Desi Arnaz*. New York: William Morrow and Company, 1993.

Taylor, Ella. *Prime-Time Families: Television Culture in Post-War America*. Berkeley: University of California Press, 1989.

Waldron, Vince. *Classic Sitcoms: A Celebration of the Best in Prime Time Comedy*. New York: Macmillan, 1987.

Wolff, Jurgen. *Successful Sitcom Writing*. New York: St. Martin's Press, 1988.

CRITICISM
AND THEORY

Television is the most important entertainment and news medium of the second half of the twentieth century. Television criticism attempts to provide interpretation and evaluation, and theory attempts to provide conceptual maps for understanding the medium in its various contexts.

The purposes of television criticism vary. Some criticism is meant primarily for mass entertainment, such as to advise readers about whether or not they might want to watch particular upcoming programs. Other criticism is more scholarly and directed at specific audiences, such as media studies students or government policy-makers. There are many non-mutually exclusive approaches to television criticism. For example, people who engage in television criticism may employ one or more of the following types of criticism:

impressionistic—analyzes how the television program affects the critic
moral—evaluates television-related issues in relation to a particular value system
historical—examines television within the context of a period (time frame)
formal—analyzes television messages in terms of the genre to which it belongs
structural—analyzes details of the parts of a message in relationship to the whole
textual—analyzes form and content to explore how meaning is derived from myths, symbols, archetypes, etc.
production—analyzes how production variables contribute to meaning and aesthetic pleasure
sociological—studies the significance of television as part of the cultural output of a particular political and economic system

Theoretical orientations to the study of television can be superficially divided into three basic approaches—psychological, sociological, and cultural. Psychological approaches tend to concentrate on the influence of television on the individual. Sociological approaches focus on the influence of television on social groups as well as on the medium itself as a significant social institution. Cultural studies look at television as a meaning-making activity in which *texts* (programs, commercials, music videos, etc.) are created and interpreted within cultural contexts.

(See all other categories, especially Psychological Aspects and Social Aspects)

Topic Suggestions

Comparative analysis of television criticism in newspapers and on television
Comparative analysis of television with other forms of communication
Establishing criteria for evaluating the influence of television
Evolution of critical approaches to the scholarly study of television
Evolution of psychological, sociological, and cultural theories toward understanding television
History of television criticism
How can you, the viewer, get the most out of the television experience?
If you could go back and start from scratch, how would you create your *perfect* television system?
Living without television
Meaning and morality on television
The medium is the message: television in the theories of Marshall McLuhan
Ratings vs. responsibility: television and the public interest
The relationship between meanings on television and the social relations of television production
The significance of television as a mass medium in the twentieth century
Television: transmitting emotions and visual images more effectively than ideas and ideologies
Television and cultural homogenization
Television and the concept of cultural heroes
Television and the concept of power
Television and the concept of time
Television as cultural storyteller (myth-maker)

Sources

Allen, Robert C., ed. *Channels of Discourse, Reassembled: Television and Contemporary Criticism.* 2nd ed. Chapel Hill, NC: University of North Carolina Press, 1992.
Arlen, Michael J. *The Camera Age: Essays on Television.* New York: Farrar, Straus & Giroux, 1981.

Avery, Robert K. and David Eason, eds. *Critical Perspectives on Media and Society*. New York: Guilford Press, 1991.

Berger, Arthur Asa. *Media Analysis Techniques*. Rev. ed. Newbury Park, CA: Sage, 1991.

Bianculli, David. *Teleliteracy: Taking Television Seriously*. New York: Continuum, 1992.

Bryant, Jennings and Dolf Zillmann, eds. *Media Effects: Advances in Theory and Research*. Hillsdale, NJ: Lawrence Erlbaum Associates, 1994.

Butler, Jeremy. *Analyzing Television: Critical Methods and Applications*. Belmont, CA: Wadsworth, 1994.

Carey, James W., ed. *Media Myths and Narratives: TV and the Press*. Beverly Hills, CA: Sage, 1988.

Cooper, Thomas. *Television and Ethics: A Bibliography*. New York: Mac-Millan, 1988.

Curran, James, et al. *Impacts and Influences: Essays on Media Power in the Twentieth Century*. London: Methuen, 1987.

Comstock, George. *The Evolution of American Television*. Newbury Park, CA: Sage, 1989.

D'Agostino, Peter and David Tafler, eds. *Transmission: Toward a Post-Television Culture*. Thousand Oaks, CA: Sage, 1994.

Davis, Douglas. *The Five Myths of Television Power or Why the Medium Is Not the Message*. New York: Simon & Schuster, 1993.

Eberwein, Robert. *Film and Television: New Approaches to Theory and Criticism*. Metuchen, NJ: Scarecrow Press, 1994.

Enright, D. J. *Fields of Vision: Essays on Literature, Language, and Television*. New York: Oxford University Press, 1989.

"Ferment in the Field." Special issue of *Journal of Communication* (Summer 1983).

Fiske, John. *Television Culture*. New York: Methuen, 1987.

Fiske, John and John Hartley. *Reading Television*. London: Methuen, 1978.

Forsberg, Geraldine E. *Critical Thinking in an Image World: Alfred Korzybski's Theoretical Principles Extended to Critical Television Evaluation*. Lanham, MD: University Press of America, 1993.

Gitlin, Todd. *Inside Prime Time*. New York: Pantheon, 1983.

Gitlin, Todd, ed. *Watching Television*. New York: Pantheon, 1986.

Goldsen, Rose K. *The Show and Tell Machine: How Television Works and Works You Over*. New York: Dial, 1977.

Goodwin, Andrew and Garry Whannel, eds. *Understanding Television*. New York: Routledge, 1990.

Hartley, John. *Tele-ology: Studies in Television*. London: Routledge, 1992.

Henderson, Katherine U. and Joseph A. Mazzeo, eds. *Meanings of the Medium: Perspectives on the Art of Television*. Westport, CT: Praeger, 1990.

Himmelstein, Hal. *On the Small Screen: New Approaches in Television and Video Criticism*. New York: Praeger, 1981.

Himmelstein, Hal. *TV Myth and the American Mind*. 2nd ed. New York: Praeger, 1994.

Jacobson, Ronald L. *Television-Related Cartoons in The New Yorker Magazine: Over 1250 Cartoon Descriptions (1950–1990) Indexed by Cartoonist and Subject*. Jefferson, NC: McFarland, 1993.

Kaplan, E. Ann, ed. *Regarding TV*. Los Angeles: American Film Institute, 1983.

Lichter, Robert S. *Watching America: What Television Tells Us About Our Lives*. New York: Prentice Hall, 1991.

Limburg, Val. *Electronic Media Ethics*. Boston: Focal Press, 1994.

Lodziak, Conrad. *The Power of Television: A Critical Appraisal*. New York: St. Martin's Press, 1986.

McKibben, Bill. *The Age of Missing Information*. New York: Random House, 1992.

McQuail, Denis. *Mass Communication Theory: An Introduction*. Beverly Hills, CA: Sage, 1993.

Mander, Gerry. *Four Arguments for the Elimination of Television*. New York: William Morrow, 1978.

Mankiewicz, Frank and Joel Swerdlow. *Remote Control: Television and the Manipulation of American Life*. New York: Ballantine Books, 1978.

Marc, David. *Demographic Vistas: TV in American Culture*. Philadelphia: University of Pennsylvania Press, 1984.

Mellencamp, Patricia, ed. *Logics of Television: Essays in Cultural Criticism*. Bloomington: University of Indiana Press, 1990.

Newcomb, Horace, ed. *Television: The Critical View*. 5th ed. New York: Oxford University Press, 1994.

Olson, Alan, Christoper Parr and Deborah Parr. *Video Icons & Values*. New York: SUNY Press, 1991.

Orlik, Peter B. *Critiquing Radio and Television Content*. Boston: Allyn and Bacon, 1988.

Papazian, Ed. *Medium Rare: The Evolution, Workings & Impact of Commercial Television*. Rev. ed. New York: Media Dynamics, 1989.

Parenti, Michael. *Make-Believe Media: The Politics of Entertainment*. New York: St. Martin's Press, 1992.

Perkinson, Henry J. *Getting Better: Television and Moral Progress*. New Brunswick: Transaction Publishers, 1991.

Phelan, John. *Disenchantment: Meaning and Morality in the Media*. New York: Hastings House, 1980.

Phelan, John. *Mediaworld: Programming the Public*. New York: Seabury Press, 1977.

Philo, Greg. *Seeing and Believing: The Influence of Television*. London: Routledge, 1990.

Postman, Neil. *Amusing Ourselves to Death: Public Discourse in the Age of Show Business*. New York: Viking, 1985.

Powers, Ron. *The Beast, the Eunuch and the Glass-Eyed Child: Television in the '80s*. San Diego: Harcourt Brace Jovanovich, 1990.

Prouty, Howard H., ed. *Variety Television Reviews, 1923–1988*. New York: Garland Publishing, 1989.

Real, Michael. *Super Media: A Cultural Studies Approach*. Beverly Hills, CA: Sage, 1989.

Root, Janet. *Open the Box: About Television*. New York: Routledge, 1988.

Shoemaker, Pamela and Stephen Reese. *Mediating the Message: Theories of Influences on Mass Media Content*. New York: Longman, 1991.

Silverstone, Roger. *Television and Everyday Life*. New York: Routledge, 1994.

Sklar, Robert. *Prime-Time America: Life on and Behind the Television Screen*. New York: Oxford University Press, 1980.

Stein, Benjamin. *The View from Sunset Boulevard: America as Brought to You by the People Who Make Television*. New York: Basic Books, 1979.

Tannenbaum, Percy H., ed. *The Entertainment Functions of Television*. Hillsdale, NJ: Lawrence Erlbaum, 1980.

Tichi, Cecilia. *Electronic Hearth: Creating an American Television Culture*. New York: Oxford University Press, 1991.

Vande Berg, Leah and Lawrence Wenner, eds. *Television Criticism: Approaches and Applications*. New York: Longman, 1992.

Williams, Raymond. *Television: Technology and Cultural Form*. London: Fontana, 1975.

Zettl, Herb. *Sight, Sound, Motion: Applied Media Aesthetics*. 2nd ed. Belmont, CA: Wadsworth, 1990.

DRAMA

Television drama has been a popular staple of the medium since its inception. Already proven popular in theaters, movies, and on radio, dramatic programs were readily enjoyed via the new television medium during the 1950s. High-quality live dramatic anthology series, such as *Playhouse 90,* contributed to what we now call television's *golden years.* Then and now, the nature of television drama is conflict which is expressed through characters, dialogue, and plots. Television drama functions for some viewers as a means of diversion or escape, and for others it is a fictional representation of realistic human relationships and social behavior. Conventional dramatic formats include the television movie, the weekly series, the miniseries, and the weekday soap opera.

Today, dramatic television in the United States is largely produced by independent companies that enter into contractual agreements with networks. Over the years, some producers have been very successful in creating popular dramatic programming. For example, Aaron Spelling has produced several hit series, including *Mod Squad, Love Boat,* and *Beverly Hills 90210.* The costs of producing prime time dramatic programs is high, and most dramatic series are deficit-financed, meaning that they cost more to produce than the initial licensing fee paid by a network for their first run. Additional revenue and profit come from reruns and from syndication in the international market, where U.S. television dramas are valued for their high production values and commercial viability.

Daytime serials, better known as soap operas, are among the most avidly viewed programs on television. Attractive actors, topical issues, and never-ending storylines attract viewers back weekday after weekday. Some scholars suggest other reasons for the popularity of soap operas are that they offer a sense of community and the promise of hope to viewers.

Other dramatic television genres include westerns, historical dramas, crime-detective programs, mysteries, adventures, science fiction, and docudramas. A relatively new hybrid is the *dramedy*, such as *Northern Exposure,* which combines elements of drama with comedy.

(See also Movies, Production, Programming)

Topic Suggestions

Cinéma verité production techniques and crime dramas
Comparative analysis of daytime soap operas and prime time dramas
Comparative analysis of dramatic structure and content of U.S. soap operas
    with soap operas in one or more other countries
Comparative analysis of television drama on commercial television and
    PBS
Cultural significance of television drama in the United States
Depiction of sexual relations on soap operas
Depiction of women in television drama
Dramedy: a hybrid genre blending drama and comedy
Economic analysis of producing a dramatic television series
Historical analysis of iconography in the television western series
Historical analysis of the *Hallmark Hall of Fame* television drama special
    presentations
History of depiction of sex and violence in television dramas
History of soap company production and sponsorship of soap operas
How television drama deals with death and dying
How television drama deals with health issues (e.g., AIDS or alcohol abuse)
Live television dramas during television's "golden years"
Moral values in television drama
Parasocial interaction with soap opera actors
Portrayals of the elderly in television drama
Profile of the soap opera audience
Racial relations in television drama
Recreating real-life drama in docudramas
Resolution of moral dilemmas on soap operas
Review of the research literature on the impact of antisocial behavior in
    television drama on young viewers
The significance of community in soap operas
Soap Opera Digest and other publications that cover television soap operas
Sociocultural influences of soap operas in developing countries
Television drama genres
The transition of soap operas from radio to television
Uses and gratifications of soap opera viewers
Why are U.S. television dramas popular in many countries?

Sources

Allen, Robert C. *Speaking of Soap Operas*. Chapel Hill: University of North Carolina Press, 1985.

Anderegg, Michael, ed. *Inventing Vietnam: The War in Film and Television*. Philadelphia: Temple University Press, 1991.

Ang, Ien. *Watching Dallas: Soap Opera and Melodramatic Imagination*. New York: Methuen, 1985.

Averson, Richard, compiler. *Electronic Drama: Television Plays of the Sixties*. Boston: Beacon Press, 1971.

Bennett, Tony, ed. *Popular Fiction: Technology, Ideology, Production, Reading*. London: Routledge, 1990.

Brandt, George W. *British Television Drama in the 1980s*. New York: Cambridge University Press, 1993.

Brown, Mary Ellen. *Soap Opera and Women's Talk*. Thousand Oaks, CA: Sage, 1994.

Buckman, Peter. *All for Love: A Study in Soap Opera*. London: Secker & Warburg, 1984.

Buxton, David. *From the Avengers to Miami Vice: Form and Ideology in Television Series*. Manchester, England: Manchester University Press, 1990.

Buxton, Rodney. "'After It Happened...': The Battle to Present AIDS in Television Drama," in *Television: The Critical View*. 5th ed. Edited by Horace Newcomb. New York: Oxford University Press, 1994.

Cantor, Muriel G. and Suzanne Pingree. *The Soap Opera*. Newbury Park, CA: Sage, 1983.

Cassata, Mary and Thomas Skill. *Life on Daytime Television: Tuning in American Serial Drama*. Norwood, NJ: Ablex, 1983.

Frentz, Suzanne, ed. *Staying Tuned: Contemporary Soap Opera Criticism*. Bowling Green, OH: Bowling Green State University Popular Press, 1992.

Gerbner, George and Nancy Signorielli. *Women and Minorities in Television Drama, 1969-1978: A Research Report*. Philadelphia: University of Pennsylvania Annenenberg School of Communication, 1979.

Gianakos, Larry J. *Television Drama Series Programming: A Comprehensive Chronicle, 1984-1986*. Metuchen, NJ: Scarecrow Press, 1992.

Gianakos, Larry J. *Television Drama Series Programming*. 5 vols. Metuchen, NJ: Scarecrow Press, 1978-1987.

Greenberg, Bradley S. *Life on Television: Content Analyses of U.S. TV Drama*. Norwood, NJ: Ablex, 1980.

Hawes, William. *American Television Drama: The Experimental Years*. Birmingham: University of Alabama Press, 1986.

Intintoli, James. *Taking Soaps Seriously: The World of Guiding Light*. New York: Praeger, 1984.

Jarvik, Laurence. *Masterpiece Theatre and the Politics of Quality*. Metuchen, NJ: Scarecrow Press, 1995.

Kaminsky, Stuart M. and Jeffrey H. Mahan. *American Television Genres.* Chicago: Nelson-Hall, 1985.

Klobas, Lauri E. *Disability Drama in Television and Film.* Jefferson, NC: McFarland, 1988.

La Guardia, Robert. *Soap World.* New York: Arbor House, 1983.

Landy, Marcia, ed. *Imitations of Life: A Reader of Film and Television Melodrama.* Detroit: Wayne State University Press, 1991.

Larka, Robert. *Television's Private Eye: An Examination of Twenty Years of Programming of a Particular Genre, 1949–1969.* New York: Arno, 1973.

Levinson, Richard and William Link. *Stay Tuned... An Inside Look at the Making of Prime-Time Television.* New York: St. Martin's Press, 1981.

Lichter, Linda S. and S. Robert Lichter. *Prime Time Crime: Criminals and Law Enforcers in TV Entertainment.* Washington, DC: Media Institute, 1983.

McNeil, Alex. *Total Television: A Comprehensive Guide to Programming from 1948 to the Present.* Updated 3rd ed. New York: Penguin, 1994.

Nariman, Heidi Noel. *Soap Operas for Social Change: Toward a Methodology for Entertainment-Education Television.* Westport: CT: Greenwood Publishing, 1993.

Nochimson, Martha. *No End to Her: Soap Opera and the Female Subject.* Berkeley: University of California Press, 1992.

Perse, Elizabeth M. "Soap Opera Viewing Patterns of College Students and Cultivation." *Journal of Broadcasting and Electronic Media* (Spring 1986): 175–93.

Rosenthal, Alan. *Writing Docudrama: Dramatizing Reality for Film and TV.* Boston: Focal Press, 1994.

Rouverol, Jean. *Writing for Daytime Drama.* Boston: Focal Press, 1992.

Schemering Christopher. *The Soap Opera Encyclopedia.* New York: Ballantine Books, 1985.

Sparks, Richard. *Television and the Drama of Crime: Moral Tales and the Place of Crime in Public Life.* Buckingham, England: Open University Press, 1992.

Stempel, Tom. *Storytellers to the Nation: A History of American Television Writing.* New York, Continuum, 1992.

Tannenbaum, Percy H., ed. *The Entertainment Functions of Television.* Hillsdale, NJ: Lawrence Erlbaum, 1980.

Thompson, Robert J. *Adventures on Prime Time: The Television Programs of Stephen J. Cannell.* Westport, CT: Praeger, 1990.

Thorburn, David. "Television Melodrama," in *Television: The Critical View.* 5th ed. Edited by Horace Newcomb. New York: Oxford University Press, 1994.

Tulloch, John. *Television Drama: Agency, Audience and Myth.* London: Routledge, 1990.

Turow, Joseph. *Playing Doctor: TV, Storytelling, and Medical Power.* Oxford: Oxford University Press, 1989.

Vande Berg, Leah and Nick Trujillo. *Organizational Life on Television.*
Norwood, NJ: Ablex, 1989.
West, Richard. *Television Westerns: Major and Minor Series, 1946–1978.*
Jefferson, NC: McFarland, 1987.

EDUCATION

From television's beginnings, some people felt that the medium should be used to educate. Education groups lobbied for channel reservations, and in 1952 the FCC reserved 242 channels for noncommercial educational broadcasting. Although there were earlier experiments and projects at other institutions, in 1953 the University of Houston's KUHT became the first educational station to go on the air on a reserved frequency.

In the 1950s, most educational stations were on the air for only a few hours each week because of lack of programs and the high costs of operation. In the early 1960s, educational programming became more readily available through National Educational Television (NET), a pseudo-network funded in large part by the Ford Foundation. The world of educational stations changed dramatically as a result of the 1967 report by the Carnegie Commission, which led to the creation of the Public Broadcasting Service (PBS). Today, most educational stations are affiliated with PBS.

In terms of programming, there are a couple important distinctions made in the research associated with this conceptual category. Educational television (ETV) programming refers to cultural material and general educational material. Instructional television (ITV) refers primarily to programming designed to teach students either in the classroom or at home. However, programs such as *This Old House* also fall under the category of instructional television because they teach particular skills. ITV plays a substantial role in some educational institutions, where it can take the form of telecourses, distance learning, and/or interactive video. Cable and satellite technology have led to more ETV and ITV, ranging from The Learning Channel cable network to Channel One, a direct broadcast satellite program (with commercials) available to schools nationwide. Much research has focused on how and what individuals learn from ETV and ITV. Controversy continues about the effectiveness of ITV versus traditional forms of learning.

A growing movement is to teach people about the television medium itself. Television literacy, part of a larger educational movement known as "media literacy," involves learning and critical thinking about the nature, business, and messages of the medium. The goals of television literacy include: 1) understanding how messages are constructed (the relation of form to content), 2) understanding the structure, financial support systems, and regulations of the television industry so as to be aware of the parameters within which producers create mediated messages, and 3) being able to critically evaluate the various forms of television content for values and ideological significance. Proponents of media literacy education believe that individuals who develop critical viewing skills will be empowered to better negotiate the impact of television messages on their personal and social lives.

(See also Children, Public Television)

Topic Suggestions

Analysis of production values for ITV programs
Basic theoretical assumptions of television literacy education
Cable in the classroom (e.g., C-SPAN in the Classroom program)
Case study of educational considerations in Children's Television Workshop production of *Sesame Street*
Case study of how educational television is used in a local school system
Case study of how television literacy is taught in a local school
Channel One (commercially sponsored news program in the classroom)
Comparative analysis of television literacy efforts in the U.S. and in one or more other countries
Distance learning
Educational applications of commercial television entertainment programs
The educational value of children's videos (e.g., *Barney*) for pre-schoolers
History of technology for delivering educational television into the classroom
History of television literacy education
History of the use of educational television in higher education
How do students learn best from television?
Instructional uses of closed captioning systems in television and video
Interactive educational/instructional video (convergence of computer, telephone, and video technologies)
Is there a significant relationship between reading skills and television viewing behavior?
The Learning Channel
Literature review of learning effectiveness studies of educational and/or instructional television

National Educational Television (NET as the forerunner to public television)

Organizational history of the National Association of Educational Broadcasters (NAEB)

PBS commitment to educational and instructional television programming

Pedagogical considerations in using video in the classroom

Position paper for or against formal television literacy curricula in public schools

Regulatory history of noncommercial educational television broadcasting

The role of television in teaching reading

Training teachers to effectively utilize television in the classroom

Use of instructional television in teaching English as a second language

Use of instructional video in training programs (e.g., law enforcement)

What are the necessary ingredients for a successful telecourse?

Sources

Alvarado, Manuel and Oliver Boyd-Barrett, eds. *Media Education: An Introduction*. London: BFI, 1992.

Alvarado, Manuel, et al. *Learning the Media: An Introduction to Media Teaching*. London: Macmillan Education Ltd., 1987.

Anderson, Neil. *Media Works*. London: Oxford University Press, 1989.

Bazalgette, Cary. *Primary Media Education: A Curriculum Statement*. London: British Film Institute, 1989.

Bazalgette, Cary, Evelyne Bevort and Josiane Savino, eds. *New Directions: Media Education Worldwide*. London: British Film Institute, 1992.

Blakely, Robert J. *To Serve the Public Interest: Educational Broadcasting in the United States*. Syracuse, NY: Syracuse University Press, 1979.

Bowker, Julian. *Secondary Media Education: A Curriculum Statement*. London: British Film Institute, 1991.

Brown, James A. *Television "Critical Viewing Skills" Education: Major Media Literacy Projects in the United States and Selected Countries*. Hillsdale, NJ: Lawrence Erlbaum Associates, 1991.

Buckingham, David. *Watching Media Learning: Making Sense of Media Education*. London: Falmer Press/Taylor & Francis, 1990.

Clarke, Mike. *Teaching Popular TV*. London: Heinemann, 1987.

Dennis, Everette E. and Craig L. LaMay, eds. *America's Schools and the Mass Media*. New Brunswick, NJ: Transaction, 1993.

Downing, John and others. *Questioning the Media: A Critical Introduction*. Newbury Park, CA: Sage, 1990.

Elmore, Garland C. *The Communication Disciplines in Higher Education: A Guide to Academic Programs in the United States and Canada*. Murray, KY: Association for Communication Administration, 1990.

Hays, Kim, ed. *TV, Science, and Kids: Teaching our Children to Question*. Reading, MA: Addison-Wesley, 1984.

Hudspeth, D.R. and Ronald G. Brey. *Instructional Telecommunications: Principles and Applications*. Westport, CT: Greenwood, 1985.

Johnstone, Jerome. *Electronic Learning from Audiotape to Videodisc*. Hillsdale, NJ: Lawrence Erlbaum Associates, 1988.

Lochte, Robert H. *Interactive Television and Instruction*. Englewood Cliffs, NJ: Educational Technology Publications, 1993.

Lusted, David. *The Media Studies Book*. London: Routledge, 1991.

Masterman, Len. *Teaching About TV*. London: Comedia, 1985.

Masterman, Len. *Teaching the Media*. London: Routledge, 1990.

Murray, Michael D. and Anthony J. Fewrri. *Teaching Mass Communication: A Guide to Better Instruction*. New York: Praeger, 1992.

Nivens, Harold. *Broadcast Programs in American Colleges and Universities*. 16th Report. Washington, DC: Broadcast Education Association, 1986.

Ontario Ministry of Education. *Media Literacy: Resource Guide*. Government of Ontario Bookstore Publications, 1989.

Pintoff, Ernest. *The Complete Guide to American Film Schools & Cinema & Television Courses*. New York: Viking Penguin, 1994.

Singer, Dorothy G., Jerome Singer and Diana Zuckerman. *Teaching Television: How to Use TV to Your Children's Advantage*. New York: Dial, 1981.

Unwin, D. and P. McAleese. *The Encyclopedia of Educational Media Communications and Technology*. 2nd ed. Westport, CT: Greenwood Press, 1988.

Wood, Donald and Donald G. Wylie. *Educational Telecommunications*. Belmont, CA: Wadsworth, 1977.

Zigerell, James. *The Uses of Television in American Higher Education*. Westport, CT: Greenwood Press, 1991.

HISTORY

This category is meant to include both the history of television and television's coverage and portrayal of historical events. Studying the history of the medium allows one to gain better perspective of the present through an understanding of the past.

At the 1939 World's Fair, Americans got their first glimpse of a device that would become in the second half of the 20th century the major source of both leisure time entertainment and information about the world. During five decades, television has evolved in terms of design, distribution, production, content, regulation, and so on. This history of television is relatively short but one rich in detail in this age of information. Like most histories, the history of television is about human achievements and change. Television history is primarily about people, events, technological innovations, trends, ideas, and underlying principles.

Television by its very nature is a historical medium. That is, television chronicles history, transmitting and recording live events such as the Kennedy assassination and the first man walking on the moon. Television also presents well-researched documentaries and slickly-produced docudramas which re-present history for mass audiences. For example, research has suggested that the popular "Holocaust" mini-series, attended to by millions of Americans in the 1970s, provided a significant number of viewers with new historical insight about World War II. Television's influence on history can also be appreciated through its relationship to politics, including coverage of political conventions, presidential debates, political advertising, and Congressional hearings.

(See also News, Politics, Programming)

Topic Suggestions

Biographical study of a television pioneer (e.g., David Sarnoff or Philo Farnsworth)

Blacklisting and the television industry
Case history of the evolution of a particular program genre (e.g., soap opera, talk shows, religious programming, etc.)
Chronological analysis of a particular decade in the evolution of television
The Civil War — A case study of a historical documentary on PBS
Coast to coast: the history of television production in New York and Hollywood
Comparative analysis of television coverage of public health issues across four decades
Comparative analysis of the beginning of television in the United States with the beginning of television in one or more other countries
A cultural history of television exploring how the medium has helped to change public conceptions of time and space
The FCC "freeze" on new television station licenses from 1948 to 1952
Historical analysis of the relationship between television regulation and the First Amendment
Historical analysis of the treatment of a social problem on television (e.g., poverty)
Historical overview of non-commercial television
Historical overview of ownership and control in the television industry
Historical overview of the economics of commercial sponsorship of network programs
History of competition between television and other media
History of live television (emphasis on television's "Golden Years")
History of major developments in television distribution technology
How television has changed our concept of history
The impact of television in the United States in the 20th century
Literature review of published histories of television
Oral histories of people involved in television's early years
The quiz show scandals
Radio and the pre-history of television
Self-reflexivity: how television looks at its own history
Television coverage of historical events
Using the television docudrama to teach history

Sources

Arlen, Michael. J. *Living Room War*. New York: The Viking Press, 1969.
Abramson, Albert. *The History of Television, 1880–1941*. Jefferson, NC: McFarland, 1987.
Altschuler, Glenn C. and David I. Grossvogel. *Changing Channels: America in TV Guide*. Urbana, IL: University of Illinois, 1992.
Anderson, Kent. *Television Fraud: The History and Implications of the Quiz Show Scandals*. Westport, CT: Greenwood Press, 1978.
Barnouw, Erik. *A Tower in Babel: A History of Broadcasting in the United*

States to 1933 (1966); *The Golden Web: A History of Broadcasting in the United States 1933-1953* (1968); *The Image Empire: A History of Broadcasting in the United States from 1953* (1970). New York: Oxford University Press, 1966-1970.

Barnouw, Erik. *Tube of Plenty: The Evolution of American Television.* 2nd ed. New York: Oxford University Press, 1990.

Bedell, Sally. *Up the Tube: Prime-Time TV and the Silverman Years.* New York: Viking, 1981.

Bibb, Porter. *It Ain't as Easy as It Looks: Ted Turner's Amazing Story.* New York: Crown, 1993.

Bilby, Kenneth. *The General: David Sarnoff and the Rise of the Communications Industry.* New York: Harper & Row, 1986.

Boddy, William. *Fifties Television: The Industry and Its Critics.* Urbana: University of Illinois Press, 1990.

Bowles, Jerry. *A Thousand Sundays: The Story of the Ed Sullivan Show.* New York: Putnam, 1980.

Castleman, Harry and Walter J. Podrazik. *Watching TV: Four Decades of American TV.* New York: McGraw Hill, 1982.

Dayan, Daniel and Elihu Katz. *Media Events: The Live Broadcasting of History.* Cambridge, MA: Harvard University Press, 1992.

Engel, Joel. *Gene Roddenberry: The Myth and the Man Behind Star Trek.* New York: Hyperion, 1994.

Farnsworth, Elma G. *Distant Vision: Romance and Discovery on an Invisible Frontier.* New York: Pemberly Kent, 1989. (Biography of the author's husband, television inventor Philo Farnsworth)

Foley, Karen Sue. *The Political Blacklist in the Broadcast Industry: The Decade of the 1950's.* New York: Arno, 1979.

Glut, Donald F. and Jim Harmon. *The Great Television Heroes.* New York: Doubleday, 1975.

Greenfield, Jeff. *Television: The First Fifty Years.* New York: Abrahms, 1987.

Halberstam, David. *The Powers That Be.* New York: Knopf, 1979.

Hay, Peter. *Canned Laughter: The Best Stories from Radio & Television's Golden Years.* New York: Oxford University Press, 1992.

Henderson, Amy. *On the Air: Pioneers of American Broadcasting.* Washington, DC: National Portrait Gallery, Smithsonian Institution, 1988.

Hilliard, Robert L. and Michael C. Keith. *The Broadcast Century: A Biography of American Broadcasting.* Boston: Focal Press, 1992.

Hofer, Stephen F. "Philo Farnsworth: Television Pioneer." *Journal of Broadcasting* (Spring 1979): 153–66.

Inglis, Andrew F. *Behind the Tube: A History of Broadcasting Technology and Business.* Boston: Focal Press, 1990.

Kraeuter, David W. *British Radio and Television Pioneers: A Patent Bibliography.* Metuchen, NJ: Scarecrow Press, 1993.

Lyon, Eugene. *David Sarnoff: A Biography.* New York: Harper, 1966.

Marc, David. *Prime Time, Prime Movers*. Boston: Little, Brown and Company, 1992.

Marling. Karal Ann. *As Seen on TV: The Visual Culture of Everyday Life in the 1950s*. Cambridge: Harvard University Press, 1994.

O'Connor, John, ed. *American History/American TV: Interpreting the Video Past*. New York: Ungar, 1983.

Ritchie, Michael. *Please Stand By: The Pre-History of Television*. New York: Penguin, 1995.

Skutch, Ira. *I Remember Television: A Memoir* (Directors Guild of America Oral History). Metuchen, NJ: Scarecrow Press, 1989.

Slide, Anthony, ed. *The Television Industry: A Historical Dictionary*. Westport, CT: Greenwood Press, 1991.

Smith, Sally Bedell. *In All His Glory: The Life of William S. Paley, the Legendary Tycoon and His Brilliant Circle*. New York: Simon and Schuster, 1990.

Spigel, Lynn. *Make Room for TV: Television and the Family Ideal in Postwar America*. Chicago: University of Chicago Press, 1992.

Stempel, Tom. *Storytellers to the Nation: A History of American Television Writing*. New York: Continuum, 1992. Sterling, Christopher H. and John M. Kittross. *Stay Tuned: A Concise History of American Broadcasting*. 2nd ed. Belmont, CA: Wadsworth, 1990.

Sturcken, Frank. *Live Television: The Golden Age of 1946–1958 in New York*. Jefferson, NC: McFarland, 1990.

Udelson, Joseph H. *The Great Television Race: A History of the American Television Industry 1925–1941*. Tuscaloosa AL: University of Alabama Press, 1982.

Watson, Mary Ann. *The Expanding Vista: American Television in the Kennedy Years*. New York: Oxford University Press, 1990.

Weaver, Pat with Thomas M. Coffey. *The Best in the House: The Golden Years of Radio and Television*. New York: Alfred A. Knopf, 1994.

Wilk, Max. *The Golden Age of Television: Notes From the Survivors*. Wakefield, RI: Moyer Bell Limited, 1990.

Winship, Michael. *Television*. New York: Random House, 1988.

Wyver, John. *The Moving Image: An International History of Film, Television & Video*. Oxford: Blackwell Publishers, 1989.

INDUSTRY

The television industry ranges from production of programs to distribution businesses to the manufacturing of television sets and VCRs for home reception. Therefore, one should appreciate the television industry as composed of several industries that sometimes have conflicting interests (e.g., broadcasting and cable). Similar to other industries, the television industry is influenced by, among other factors, general economic conditions, technological developments, its own organizational structures, management/labor relations, the regulatory climate, consumer preferences, and competition in the marketplace.

The television industry in the United States is characterized by its largely commercial nature, its mostly private ownership, and its localized distribution structure (i.e., local broadcast stations and cable systems). Ownership and control in the television industry, from television stations to production companies, have shifted increasingly over the years from independent to corporate conglomerates. Today, certain parts of the television industry, including the networks, have been criticized for their oligopolistic nature.

New York and Los Angeles have long been the corporate and production centers of the industry, although in recent years, some production has moved to other locations mostly to save money on non-union labor, and some cable operations are headquartered in different parts of the country, such as TCI in Denver and CNN in Atlanta. Various television industry professional organizations, including the National Association of Broadcasters, maintain offices in Washington, D.C., where they can lobby politicians concerning their particular concerns.

In the beginning, the television industry recruited some of its work force from the radio industry and later from the motion picture industry. Today, formal training for careers in the television industry takes place in technical schools and at colleges and universities, in programs where students usually have opportunities to intern in professional workplaces such as television stations and production companies.

However, the majority of top management personnel in the television industry tend to be graduates of business schools rather than communications programs, reflecting the industry's primary purpose of producing profits.

(See also Broadcast Stations and Networks, History, Production, Programming, Regulation)

Topic Suggestions

American Federation of Radio and Television Artists (AFTRA): a case study of a television industry union

Biographical profile of a former or current television industry executive (e.g., former CBS President William Paley)

Change of ownership at the three major broadcast networks (ABC, CBS, and NBC) in the 1980s

Comparative analysis of senders' costs of distribution to deliver television messages into the home (e.g., cable vs. telephone company)

Comparative analysis of the economic aspects of pay-per-view versus traditional commercial television

Comparative analysis of the economic aspects of producing U.S. television programming in Canada versus Hollywood

Cross-media and group ownership of television stations

Economic analysis of launching a new television network

Economic analysis of the television syndication market

FCC regulation of television station ownership and control

Historical analysis of the relationship between the advertising and television industries

Historical analysis of the relationship between the broadcasting and cable television industries

Historical analysis of the relationship between the cable and telephone industries

Historical analysis of the relationship between the motion picture and television industries

Historical analysis of the relationship between the radio and television industries

History of competing technologies in the television industry

History of concentration (mergers) in the television industry

History of government regulation of the broadcast networks' financial interests in prime time programming

History of industry self-regulation

History of labor practices in the television industry

History of the television receiver (TV set) industry

How people are trained and educated (at training schools, colleges, and universities) for work in the television industry

Minority representation, ownership, and control in the television industry
The National Association of Broadcasters (NAB): a case study of a television industry lobby group
Oligopolistic and monopolistic practices in television industries
Organization and management of a medium-market broadcast television station
Survey of ownership and control of one or more television industries: broadcasting, cable, direct broadcast satellite, video, the telephone companies, etc.
The television industry and the public interest
Television programs as international commodities

Sources

Alexander, Alison, James Owers and Rod Carveth, eds. *Media Economics: Theory and Practice.* Hillsdale, NJ: Lawrence Erlbaum Associates, 1993.

Bagdikian, Ben H. *The Media Monopoly.* 4th ed. Boston: Beacon Press, 1992.

Becker, Lee, et al. *The Training and Hiring of Journalists.* Norwood, NJ: Ablex, 1987.

Bennett, James R. *Control of the Media in the United States: An Annotated Bibliography.* New York: Garland, 1992.

Blanksteen, Jane and Avi Odeni. *TV: Careers Behind the Screen.* New York: John Wiley, 1987.

Blumenthal, Howard J. *Careers in Television.* Boston: Little, Brown & Company, 1992.

Blumenthal, Howard J. and Oliver R. Goodenough. *This Business of Television.* New York: Billboard Books, 1991.

Blumler, Jay G. and T. J. Nossiter, eds. *Broadcasting Finance in Transition: A Comparative Handbook.* New York: Oxford University Press, 1991.

Brown, Les. *Television: The Business Behind the Box.* New York: Harcourt, Brace, Jovanovich, 1971.

Cantor, Muriel G. and Joel M. Cantor. *Prime-Time Television: Content and Control.* 2nd ed. Newbury Park, CA: Sage, 1992.

Denison, D. C. *As Seen on TV.* New York: Simon & Schuster, 1992.

Du Charme, Rita, compiler. *Bibliography of Media Management and Economics.* Minneapolis: Media Management and Economics Resource Center, School of Journalism and Mass Communication, University of Minnesota, 1986.

Dunnett, Peter. *The World Television Industry: An Economic Analysis.* London: Routledge, 1990.

Ellis, John. *Visible Fictions: Cinema – Television – Video.* New York: Routledge, 1992.

Garin, Michael N. and Thomas A. Redmond. "The Changing Economic Structures and Relationships Among Entertainment Industry Participants in the 21st Century," in *Television for the 21st Century: The Next Wave*. Edited by Charles M. Firestone. Washington, D.C.: The Aspen Institute, 1993.

Gould, Dantia. *The Pay-Per-View Explosion*. York, ME: QV Publishing, 1991.

Head, Sydney W. and Christopher H. Sterling. *Broadcasting in America: A Survey of Electronic Media*. 6th ed. Boston: Houghton Mifflin, 1990.

Hilliard, Robert L. *Television Station Operations and Management*. Boston, MA: Focal Press, 1989.

Howard, Herbert H. *Group and Cross-Media Ownership of Television Stations: 1988*. Washington, DC: National Association of Broadcasters, 1988.

Klein, Paul, et al. *Inside the TV Business*. New York: Sterling, 1979.

Lavine, John M. and Daniel B. Wackman. *Managing Media Organizations*. New York: Longman, 1988.

Marcus, Norman. *Broadcast and Cable Management*. Englewood Cliffs, NJ: Prentice-Hall, 1986.

Mosco, Vincent. *Broadcasting in the United States: Innovative Challenge and Organizational Control*. Norwood, NJ: Ablex, 1979.

National Association of Broadcasters. *Television Financial Report*. Washington, DC: NAB. Annual.

Noam, Eli M., ed. *Video Media Competition: Regulation, Economics, and Technology*. New York: Columbia University Press, 1985.

Owen, Bruce M. and Steven S. Wilman. *Video Economics*. Cambridge, MA: Harvard University Press, 1992.

Picard, Robert. *Media Economics: Concepts and Issues*. Beverly Hills: Sage, 1989.

Powell, Jon T. and Wally Gair, eds. *Public Interest and the Business of Broadcasting: The Broadcast Industry Looks at Itself*. Westport, CT: Greenwood Press, 1988.

Pringle, Peter K., Michael F. Starr and William E. McCavitt. *Electronic Media Management*. 3rd ed. Boston: Focal Press, 1994.

Rachlin, Harvey. *The TV and Movie Business: An Encyclopedia of Careers, Technologies, and Practices*. New York: Harmony Books, 1991.

Reed, Maxine and Robert M. Reed. *Career Opportunities in Television, Cable and Radio*. 3rd ed. New York: Facts on File, 1990.

Shanks, Bob. *The Cool Fire: How to Make It in Television*. New York: W.W. Norton, 1976.

Sherman, Barry L. *Telecommunications Management: The Broadcast and Cable Industries*. New York: McGraw-Hill, 1987.

Tartikoff, Brandon and Charles Leerhsen. *The Last Great Ride*. New York: Random House, 1992.

Tunstall, Jeremy and Michael Palmer. *Media Moguls*. London: Routledge, 1991.

Turow, Joseph. *Media Industries: The Production of News and Entertainment*. New York: Longman, 1984.

Turow, Joseph. *Media Systems in Society: Understanding Industries, Strategies, and Power*. New York: Longman, 1992.

Vogel, Harold L. *Entertainment Industry Economics: A Guide for Financial Analysis*. 2nd ed. New York: Cambridge University Press, 1990.

INTERNATIONAL

For most of the countries of the world, television is an international medium because programs are imported and/or exported, and signals cross national borders. International television can also take place through such means as co-productions, satellite links, and video cassette distribution. International television contributes to theorist Marshall McLuhan's concept of an electronic "global village." Member countries of this "global village" meet regularly through such organizations as the International Telecommunications Union (ITU) to work out satellite orbit assignments, international technical standards, and so on.

   When the subject of international television is raised, the reference is not always to communication between countries but sometimes to television in individual countries outside the United States. In every country in the world where television exists, it exists within a unique media system that is characterized largely by political philosophies and cultural values. Therefore, it is essential to develop a set of criteria for comparative analysis of television in different countries. Sydney Head, in *World Broadcasting Systems*, offers the following evaluative criteria for studying media systems: ownership, access, law and regulation, financial support, facilities, media content, audience research, and external services.

For example, ownership of television production and distribution, whether government-controlled, private, or a combination of the two, can make a large difference in the nature of television in a particular country. Television in Cuba is government-controlled and used mostly for furthering national goals, while television in the United States is largely privately-owned and operated for commercial profit.

Another way that researchers analyze television on a global level is to divide the world's countries into broader classifications based on political orientation, level of industrialization, and/or geographical location. For example, for decades it was popular to talk of television in the First World (advanced, mostly western democratic countries),

Second World (Communist countries), and the Third World (developing countries). With the collapse of the Soviet Union and communism, this classification scheme has given way to "developed" and "developing" countries.

There is a significant disparity in several television-related areas between developed and developing countries. For example, in terms of access, the 1990 *UNESCO Statistical Yearbook* suggests that while there are about 485 television receivers per 1,000 people in developed countries, there are only 44 receivers per 1,000 people in developing countries. Likewise, developing countries depend to a large extent on imported television programming, much of it from the United States.

U.S. television exports include news (especially CNN), sports programming, entertainment series, movie packages for television, programming formats (e.g., *Wheel of Fortune*), and movies-made-for-television that are released theatrically in other countries. In terms of official government-sponsored external services, the United States Information Agency operates Worldnet, a television satellite programming service available to any country that wants it.

Topic Suggestions

Analysis of news reporting styles on *CNN World Report*
Analysis of the consequences of the flow of television programming from industrialized to developing countries
Canada's border problems: U.S. television and its own cultural identity
Comparative analysis of censorship practices in two or more countries
Comparative analysis of financial support systems for public television in two or more countries
Comparative analysis of quantitative and qualitative television audience research in two or more countries
Comparative analysis of the relationship between television and politics in two or more countries
Concentration and transnational ownership in the television industry
Critical analysis of the impact of satellites in delivering television programming across national boundaries
Cross-cultural analysis of television coverage of the same event
Cross-cultural analysis of the television soap opera genre
History of the relatively late development of television in South Africa
Impact of U.S. television programs in other countries
INTELSAT
International Telecommunications Union (ITU) and international television regulation
International television industry cooperation in global newsgathering
International television production

Political implications of private ownership of television in developed and
  less-developed countries
Profile of Rupert Murdoch and his international television holdings
Role of television in the socio-economic development of less-developed
  countries
Television after the fall of communism in Eastern Europe
Television and the UNESCO-sponsored MacBride Commission Report
Television and video piracy: a study of global intellectual property rights
Television in theorist Marshall McLuhan's concept of a global village
U.S. television coverage of international affairs
United States Information Agency and its Worldnet external television service

Sources

Adams, Willam C., ed. *Television Coverage of International Affairs*. Nor-
  wood, NJ: Ablex, 1982.
Alessandro, Silj. *East of Dallas: The European Challenge to American
  Television*. Bloomington: University of Indiana Press, 1988.
Avery, Robert K., ed. *Public Service Broadcasting in a Multichannel En-
  vironment: The History and Survival of an Ideal*. New York: Long-
  man, 1993.
Blumler, Jay G., ed. *Television and the Public Interest: Vulnerable Values
  in West European Broadcasting*. Newbury Park, CA: Sage, 1992.
Boyd, Douglas A. *Broadcasting in the Arab World: A Survey of the Elec-
  tronic Media in the Middle East*. 2nd ed. Ames: Iowa State University
  Press, 1993.
Boyd, Douglas A., Joseph Strauhaar and John Lent. *Videocassette
  Recorders in the Third World*. New York: Longman, 1989.
Chatterji, P.C. *Broadcasting in India*. Newbury Park: Sage, 1987.
Chen, Anne Cooper. *Games in the Global Village: A 50-Nation Study of
  Entertainment Television*. Bowling Green, OH: Bowling Green State
  University Popular Press, 1994.
Crane, Rhonda J. *The Politics of International Standards: France and the
  Color TV War*. Norwood, NJ: Ablex, 1979.
Dowmunt, Tony, ed. *Channels of Resistance: Global Television and Local
  Empowerment*. London: BFI Publishing, 1993.
Doyle, Marc. *The Future of Television: A Global Overview of Program-
  ming, Advertising, Technology and Growth*. Lincolnwood, IL: NTC,
  1993.
Dunnett, Peter. *The World Television Industry: An Economic Analysis*.
  London: Routledge, 1990.
Etzioni-Halevy, E. *National Broadcasting Under Siege: A Comparative
  Study of Australia, Britain, Israel, and West Germany*. New York: St.
  Martin's Press, 1987.
Frederick, Howard. *Global Communication & International Relations*. Bel-
  mont, CA: Wadsworth, 1993.

Ganley, Gladys D. and Oswald H. Ganley. *Global Political Fallout: The VCR's First Decade 1976–85.* Norwood, NJ: Ablex, 1987.

Hachten, William. *The Growth of Media in the Third World: African Failures, Asian Successes.* Ames: Iowa State University Press, 1993.

Head, Sydney W. *World Broadcast Systems: A Comparative Analysis.* Belmont, CA: Wadsworth 1985. Updated Notes, 1987.

Hills, Jill with Stylianos Papathanassopoulos. *The Democracy Gap: The Politics of Information and Communication Technologies in the United States and Europe.* Westport, CT: Greenwood Press, 1991.

Howell, W. J., Jr. *World Broadcasting in the Age of the Satellite: Comparative Systems, Policies, and Issues in Mass Telecommunication.* Norwood, NJ: Ablex, 1986.

Katz, Elihu and George Wedell. *Broadcasting in the Third World: Promise and Performance.* Cambridge, MA: Harvard University Press, 1977.

Kottack, Conrad Phillip. *Prime-Time Society: An Anthropological Analysis of Television and Culture.* Belmont, CA: Wadsworth, 1990. (Comparative study of television in the United States and Brazil)

Larson, James F. *Television's Window on the World: International Affairs Coverage on the U.S. Networks.* Norwood, NJ: Ablex, 1984.

Larson, James F. and Heung-Soo Park. *Global Television and the Politics of the Seoul Olympics.* Boulder, CO: Westview Press, 1993.

Lent, John A., compiler. *Bibliographic Guide to Caribbean Mass Communication.* Westport, CT: Greenwood Press, 1992.

Lent, John A., compiler. *Bibliography of Cuban Mass Communications.* Westport, CT: Greenwood Press, 1992.

Liebes, Tama and Elihu Katz. *The Export of Meaning: Cross-Cultural Readings of Dallas.* New York: Oxford University Press, 1990.

Lull, James. *China Turned On: Television, Reform, and Resistance.* London: Routledge, 1991.

Lull, James, ed. *World Familes Watch TV.* London: Sage, 1988.

Luther, Sara Fletcher. *The United States and the Direct Broadcast Satellite: The Politics of International Broadcasting in Space.* New York: Oxford University Press, 1987.

MacBride, Sean, et al. *Many Voices, One World: Report by the International Commission for the Study of Communication Problems.* Paris: UNESCO/New York: Unipub, 1980.

MacDonald, Barrie. *Broadcasting in the United Kingdom: A Guide to Information Sources.* 2nd. ed. London: Mansell, 1993.

McQuail, Denis and Karen Siune, eds. *New Media Politics: Comparative Perspectives in Western Europe.* Beverly Hills, CA: Sage, 1986.

Mitra, Ananda. *Television and Popular Culture in India: A Study of the Mahabharat.* Thousand Oaks, CA: Sage, 1993.

Negrine Ralph and Stylianos Papathanassopoulos. *The Internationalization of Television.* New York: Columbia University Press, 1990.

Noam, Eli. *Telecommunications in Europe.* New York: Oxford University Press, 1992.

Noam, Eli. *Television in Europe*. New York: Oxford University Press, 1991.

Quester, George. *The International Politics of Television*. Lexington, MA: Lexington Books, 1990.

Rogers, Everett M. and Francis Balle, eds. *The Media Revolution in America and Western Europe*. Norwood, NJ: Ablex, 1985.

Rosen, Philip T., ed. *International Handbook to Broadcasting Systems*. Westport, CT: Greenwood Press, 1988.

Schneider, Cynthia and Brian Wallis, eds. *Global Television*. New York: Wedge Press, 1988.

Siune, Karen and Wolfgang Truetzschler, eds. *Dynamics of Media Politics: Broadcast and Electronic Media in Western Europe*. Newbury Park, CA: Sage, 1992.

Skidmore, Thomas E., ed. *Television, Politics, and the Transition to Democracy in Latin America*. Baltimore: Johns Hopkins University Press, 1993.

Sterling, Christopher H. *Foreign and International Communications Systems: A Survey Bibliography*. 4th ed. Columbus, OH: Center for Advanced Study in Telecommunication, Ohio State University, 1989.

Stevenson, Robert L. *Global Communication in the Twenty-First Century*. New York: Longman, 1994.

Verna, Tony. *Global Television: How to Create Effective Television for the 1990s*. Boston: Focal Press, 1993.

Wildman, Steven. *International Trade in Films and Television Programs*. Cambridge: Dallinger Publishing, 1988.

Wood, James. *History of International Broadcasting*. London: Peter Peregrinus Ltd., 1992.

Wyver, John. *The Moving Image: An International History of Film, Television & Video*. Oxford: Blackwell Publishers, 1989.

MINORITIES

For the purposes of this broad conceptual category, minorities include racial and ethnic minorities, homosexuals, the mentally and physically challenged, and the elderly. For most of its history, television has been a mass medium largely concerned with appealing to the largest possible audiences. Consequently, minorities of all kinds have struggled for representation and accurate portrayals on television. Today, with the ongoing fragmentation of the mass audience, some minorities now produce their own programming, ranging from low-budget public access cable productions to 24-hour programming services such as the Black Entertainment Network (BET).

Blacks, the largest racial minority group in the United States, have been at the forefront of the effort to bring more minorities into television in positive roles, and they have been relatively successful compared to Asians, Hispanics, and Native Americans. *The Cosby Show* and *Oprah Winfrey* are two examples of programs that provide positive role models for African-Americans while combating decades of under-representation and negative stereotyping. Research suggests that negative television stereotypes can influence minority members' self-perceptions and also the way these minorities are perceived by other members in society.

Most minority groups continue to be underrepresented in, among other areas, ownership and management of television stations, as workers in television news operations, and as writers and producers of entertainment programming. Over the years, minority group advisory panels have worked to increase sensitivity toward the needs of minorities among members of the still largely white male-dominated television industry. There is obviously much progress still to be made.

(See also Audience, Children, Psychological Aspects, Social Aspects)

Topic Suggestions

African-Americans in television programming
Asian-Americans in television programming
Case study of the *Cosby Show* in combating racial stereotypes
Comparative analysis of issues concerning television and ethnic minorities
   in the United States with those in one or more other countries
Effects of Black stereotypes on non–Black audience members
Ethical implications of minority representation in network news programs
Gays and lesbians in television programming
Hispanics in television programming
History of the Black Entertainment Network (BET)
How can television serve as a vehicle for improving social conditions for
   minorities?
Legal implications of minority representation on and access to broadcast
   television
The mentally challenged in television programming
Minorities in a multi-channel television universe: the significance of the
   fragmentation of the mass audience
Minorities in television news
Minority access to non-broadcast television technologies
Minority employment in the television industry (including Affirmative Ac-
   tion and Equal Opportunity Employment)
Minority family imagery and interaction on television
Minority groups and public affairs programming
Minority ownership and management of television stations and networks in
   the United States
Minority-produced programming on cable public access stations
Minority religious groups in television programming
Multicultural programming on public television
Native-Americans in television programming
Non-English language television in the United States
Perceptions of ethnic minorities to television stereotypes
The physically challenged in television programming
Representation and portrayal of the elderly in television advertising
Role of minority advocacy groups in influencing television content
Television and the socialization of ethnic minority children
Television coverage of homosexuality
Television coverage of the civil rights movement in the 1960s
Television coverage of the homeless
Television viewing habits of the elderly

Sources

Barcus, Francis Earle. *Images of Life on Children's Television: Sex Roles,
   Minorities, and Families.* New York: Praeger, 1983.

Barron, Jerome A. *Freedom of the Press for Whom? The Rise of Access to the Mass Media*. Bloomington: University of Indiana Press, 1973.

Berry, Gordon L. and Claudia Mitchell-Kernan, eds. *Television and the Socialization of the Minority Child*. Chicago: Academy Press, 1982.

Bogle, Donald. *Blacks in American Film and Television: An Encyclopedia*. New York: Garland, 1988.

Bogle, Donald. *Toms, Coons, Mulattos, Mammies & Bucks*. New York: Continuum, 1991.

Brauer, Ralph. *The Horse, the Gun, and the Piece of Property: Changing Images of the TV Western*. Bowling Green: Bowling Green University Press, 1975.

Browne, Donald, Charles Firestone and Ellen Mickiewicz. *Television/ Radio News Minorities*. Queenstown, MD: Aspen Institute, 1994.

Dates, Jannette L. and William Barlow. *Split Image: African Americans in the Mass Media*. Washington: Howard University Press, 1990.

Davis, Richard H. and James A. Davis. *TV's Image of the Elderly: A Practical Guide for Change*. Lexington, MA: Lexington Books, 1985.

Doty, Alexander. *Making Things Perfectly Queer*. Minneapolis: University of Minnesota Press, 1993.

Ely, Melvin P. *The Adventures of Amos 'n' Andy: A Social History of an American Phenomenon*. New York: Free Press, 1992.

Fuller, Linda K. *The Cosby Show: Audiences, Impact, and Implications*. Westport, CT: Greenwood Press, 1992.

Gerbner, George and Nancy Signorielli. *Women and Minorities in Television Drama, 1969–1978: A Research Report*. Philadelphia: University of Pennsylvania Annenenberg School of Communication, 1979.

Gray, Herman. "Television, Black Americans, and the American Dream," in *Television: The Critical View*. 5th ed. Edited by Horace Newcomb. New York: Oxford University Press, 1994.

Greenberg, Bradley S. et al. *Mexican Americans and the Mass Media*. Norwood, NJ: Ablex, 1983.

Hamamoto, Darrell Y. *Monitored Peril: Asian Americans and the Politics of TV Representation*. Minneapolis: University of Minnesota Press, 1994.

Hill, George. *Blacks on Television: A Selectively Annotated Bibliography*. Metuchen, NJ: Scarecrow Press, 1985.

Hill, George, Lorraine Raglin and Chas Floyd Johnson. *Black Women in Television: An Illustrated History and Bibliography*. New York: Garland Publishing, 1990.

Howes, Keith. *Broadcasting It: An Encyclopaedia of Homosexuality on Film, Radio and TV in the UK 1923–1993*. London: Cassell, 1993.

Jhally, Sut and Justin Lewis. *Enlightened Racism: The Cosby Show, Audiences, and the Myth of the American Dream*. Boulder, CO: Westview Press, 1991.

MacDonald, J. Fred. *Blacks and White TV: African-Americans in Television Since 1948*. 2nd ed. Chicago: Nelson-Hall, 1992.

Miller, Randall M. and Allen Woll. *Ethnic and Racial Images in American Film and Television*. Garland, 1987.

Montgomery, Kathryn C. *Target: Prime Time—Advocacy Groups and the Struggle Over Entertainment TV*. New York: Oxford University Press, 1989.

Naficy, Hamid. *The Making of Exile Cultures: Iranian Television in Los Angeles*. Minneapolis: University of Minnesota Press, 1993.

Nielsen Media Research. *Television Viewing Among Blacks*. Northbrook, IL: Nielsen Media Research. Annual.

Riggins, Stephen Harold, ed. *Ethnic Minority Media: An International Perspective*. Newbury Park, CA: Sage, 1992.

Rubin, Bernard, ed. *Small Voices and Great Trumpets: Minorities and the Media*. New York: Praeger, 1980.

Shaheen, Jack G. *The TV Arab*. Bowling Green: Bowling Green State University Press, 1984.

Signorielli, Nancy. *Role Portrayal and Stereotyping on Television: An Annotated Bibliography of Studies Relating to Women, Minorities, Aging, Sexual Behavior, Health and Handicaps*. Westport, CT: Greenwood Press, 1985.

Silk, Catherine. *Racism and Anti-Racism in American Popular Culture*. New York: Manchester University Press, 1990.

Wilson, Clint C. *Minorities and Media: Diversity and the End of Mass Communication*. Beverly Hills: Sage, 1985.

Wolf, Michelle A. and Alfred Kielwasser, eds. *Gay People, Sex, and the Media*. New York: Haworth Press, 1991.

Woll, A. *Ethnic and Racial Images in American Film and Television*. New York: Garland, 1987.

MOVIES

Today, the television and motion picture industries share a symbiotic relationship in which one depends upon the other for continuing success. After theatrical release, motion pictures find their way onto pay-per-view television and cable movie channels, into video stores, and eventually onto commercial television. The motion picture industry relies on television to help promote its product through advertising and publicity. The television and video industries, on the other hand, depend on the motion picture industry to deliver programming that will attract millions of viewers.

Most of the large motion picture companies (e.g., Columbia, MCA-Universal, Paramount, and Disney) have television production divisions that create programming for television. In fact, since the 1980s, there has been a steady trend toward convergence of the television and motion picture industries. For example, Rupert Murdoch, principal owner of 20th Century–Fox, started the Fox television network. The TNT cable channel was launched after owner Ted Turner purchased the MGM film library.

Relations between the television and motion picture industries were not always as close. At first, the motion picture industry felt threatened by the blossoming television business. The number of television home receivers increased rapidly in the 1950s while the number of people who attended movies fell over 40 percent. Therefore, in the early years of the television, the movie studios viewed the new medium as its arch rival. However, the motion picture industry soon realized that the new medium provided a lucrative rental market for their pre-released films. Later, Columbia Pictures led the pack as the motion picture studios began producing programs for television.

Of course, not all movies on television are produced by major studios. Most movies made-for-television are the work of independent producers who have entered into contractual relationships with the television networks. Frequently, these movies are exported to other countries for their television markets or for theatrical release.

(See also Drama, Programming, Video)

Topic Suggestions

Analysis of motion picture advertising on television

Analysis of 1980s and 1990s convergence of motion picture and television industries (e.g., 20th Century–Fox)

Analysis of production values in live television coverage of the National Academy of Motion Picture Arts and Sciences (Oscar) Awards

Case study of programming strategies on the TNT cable network (mostly films from the MGM library purchased by Ted Turner)

Columbia Pictures' "Screen Gems": the first television production division

Comparative analysis of aesthetics of viewing motion pictures in large-screen theaters and on television

Computerized colorization of black-and-white motion pictures for modern television audiences

Depiction of social issues in made-for-television movies

Depiction of television in motion pictures (e.g., "Network," and "Broadcast News")

Economic analysis of the motion pictures-on-videotape industry

History of Home Box Office (HBO) and/or other pay cable movie channels

History of the made-for-television movie (telefeature)

How and why motion pictures are edited for broadcast television

How television and video technology have influenced movie-making

How the rising popularity of television changed the movie industry in the 1950s

Impact of cable and VCRs on motion picture production output

International markets for U.S. television movies

MCA and Disney's lawsuit against Sony and its Betamax videotape recording machine

Motion picture criticism on television (e.g., Gene Shalit, and Gene Siskel and Roger Ebert)

Motion picture producers and directors who have worked in both television and film (e.g., Alfred Hitchcock)

The motion picture studios' early boycott of television

Potential impact of pay-per-view movies on the video rental industry

Subtitles or dubbing: the challenge of presenting international motion pictures on U.S. television

Sources

Anderson, Christopher. *Hollywood TV: The Studio Systems in the Fifties.* Austin: University of Texas Press, 1994.

Balio, Tino, ed. *Hollywood in the Age of Television.* London: Unwin Hyman, 1990.

Bennett, Tony, et al., eds. *Popular Television and Film*. London: British Film Institute, 1981.

Dombrowski, Dennis. "Film and Television: An Analytical History of Economic and Creative Integration." Ph.D. Dissertation completed at the University of Illinois. University Microfilms, 1982.

Edgerton, Gary. "High Concept, Small Screen: Reperceiving the Industrial and Stylistic Origins of the American Made-for-TV Movie." *Journal of Popular Film and Television* 19 (3) (1991): 114–127.

Ellis, John. *Visible Fiction: Cinema, TV, Video*. London: Routledge, 1982.

Gomery, Douglas. *Shared Pleasures: A History of Movie Presentation in the United States*. University of Wisconsin Press, 1992.

Gomery, Douglas. "Television, Hollywood, and the Development of Movies Made for Television," in *Regarding Television*. Edited by E. Ann Kaplan. Frederick, MD: University Publications of America, 1983.

Hilmes, Michele. *Hollywood and Broadcasting: From Radio to Cable*. Urbana: University of Illinois Press, 1990.

Krugman, Dean M., et al. "Video Movies at Home: Are They Viewed Like Film or Like Television?" *Journalism Quarterly* (Spring/Summer 1991): 120–130.

Lardner, James. *Fast Forward: Hollywood, the Japanese and the VCR Wars*. New York: W.W. Norton, 1987.

Marill, Alvin H. *Movies Made for Television: The Telefeature and the Mini-Series 1964–1986*. New York: New York Zoetrope, 1987.

Phillips, Gene D. "Hitchcock's Forgotten Films: The Twenty Teleplays." *Journal of Popular Film and Television* 10 (2) (1982): 73–76.

Rapping, Elayne. *The Movie of the Week: Private Stories, Public Events*. Minneapolis: University of Minnesota Press, 1992.

Reed, Rex. *Rex Reed's Guide to Movies on TV and Video*. New York: Warner Books, 1992.

Schulze, Laurie. "The Made-for-TV Movie: Industrial Practice, Cultural Form, Popular Reception," in *Television: The Critical View*. 5th ed. Edited by Horace Newcomb. New York: Oxford University Press, 1994.

Sterling, Christopher H. and John M. Kittross. *Stay Tuned: A Concise History of American Broadcasting*. 2nd ed. Belmont, CA: Wadsworth, 1990.

Television Programming Source Books: Films. 3 vols. New York: BIB/Channels. Annual.

MUSIC

Music is an important aspect of most television productions. For example, music is often used in television commercials for mood enhancement or to provide a catchy rhythm that viewers might remember in association with the advertised product or service. Music is usually featured as the prelude to programs ranging from situation comedies to news and sports. Additionally, music is frequently employed in fictional programs to convey moods and emotions and as a device to foreshadow future scenes.

As a form of entertainment itself, music has been on television since the very beginning. Musical performers, from Nat King Cole to the Boston Pops Orchestra, have had their own programs. Weekly programs like *American Bandstand* and *Soul Train* have attempted to target white and black teen audiences respectively with the latest contemporary music. Variety shows, including the long-running *Ed Sullivan Show,* have featured performances ranging from opera to rock music. Television has regularly presented musical specials, including concerts and awards programs. Musical performance has also been successfully incorporated into other television entertainment genres, including comedies such as *The Monkees* and *The Partridge Family.*

Today, when people think about the relationship between music and television, most probably think about music videos on cable networks. In 1981, MTV became the first 24-hour rock music network, presenting promotional videos received from musical recording companies. Since then, other specialized music networks have emerged, including TNN, a country music channel; BET, featuring black music; and several satellite music international channels, including MTV ventures in Europe and Latin America. Indeed, the popular music industry and these television services share a mutually beneficial relationship in which each "feeds" off the other to gain greater profit.

The future of music on television will surely be more interactive. Already, a cable service exists called Video Jukebox, which allows viewers to select videos via an onscreen menu, order and pay for their selections via their telephone, and watch their selections on a local cable channel. As television, telephone and computer technologies converge further, other services will emerge, including the possibility of sampling and then renting or purchasing music instantaneously via a digital television/computer.

Topic Suggestions

Aesthetic considerations in music videos
American Bandstand: a case history of a long-running music program
Comparative analysis of MTV and other music channels
Composing music for television drama
Digitalization: the future of music on television
Economic aspects of music video production
Exporting MTV (e.g., MTV Latin America)
From lip-synching to live: an analysis of the presentation of musical performances on television
History of classical music programming on television
History of television bands and orchestras
Influence of U.S. music videos on the indigenous music in one or more developing countries
Influence of MTV on the recording industry
Influence of music videos in advertising
Influence of television on music as a performing art
Music award shows (including those created just for television)
Music on pay-per-view (e.g., concerts, Video Jukebox)
Music videos and counterculture expression
A musical group made for television: a case study of *The Monkees*
Portrayal of racial relations in music videos
Sexism on MTV: the portrayal of women in rock videos
Use of music in television advertising

Sources

Allan, Blaine. "Music Television," in *Television: Critical Methods and Applications*. By Jeremy G. Butler. Belmont, CA: Wadsworth, 1994.
Banks, Jack. *MTV*. Boulder, CO: Westview Press (forthcoming).
Denisoff, Serge. *Inside MTV*. New York: Transaction Publishers, 1990.
Frith, Simon, Andrew Goodwin and Lawrence Grossberg, eds. *Sound and Vision: The Music Video Reader*. New York: Routledge, 1993.
Gibson, Gordon and Thomas Philips. *A Manual of Television Opera Production*. Flint, MI: National Opera Association, 1973.
Goodwin, Andrew. *Dancing in the Distraction Factory: Music Television & Popular Culture*. Minneapolis: University of Minnesota Press, 1992.

Harris, Steve. *Film and Television Composers: An International Discography, 1920–1989*. Jefferson, NC: McFarland, 1992.

Harris, Steve. *Film, Television and Stage Music on Phonograph Records: A Discography*. Jefferson, NC: McFarland, 1988.

Kaplan, E. Ann. *Rocking Around the Clock: Music TV, Postmodernism, and Consumer Culture*. New York: Methuen, 1987.

Lewis, Lisa A. "Form and Female Authorship in Music Video," in *Television: The Critical View*. 5th ed. Edited by Horace Newcomb. New York: Oxford University Press, 1994. Lewis, Lisa A. *Gender Politics and MTV: Voicing the Difference*. Philadelphia: Temple University Press, 1990.

Limbacher, James L. *Film Music: From Violins to Videos*. Metuchen, NJ: Scarecrow Press, 1974.

Lull, James, ed. *Popular Music and Communication*. Newbury Park, Ca: Sage, 1991.

Seidman, Steven A. "An Investigation of Sex-Role Stereotyping in Music Videos." *Journal of Broadcasting & Electronic Media* (Spring 1992): 209–216.

Shore, Michael. *The History of American Bandstand: It's Got a Great Beat and You Can Dance to It*. New York: Ballantine Books, 1985.

Shore, Michael. *Music Video: A Consumer's Guide*. New York: Ballantine, 1987.

Shore, Michael. *The Rolling Stone Book of Rock Video*. New York: Quill, 1984.

Skiles, Martin. *Music Scoring for TV and Motion Pictures*. Blue Ridge Summit, PA: TAB Books, 1976.

Tagg, Philip. *Kojak — 50 Seconds of Television Music: Toward the Analysis of Affect in Popular Music*. Gothenburg, Sweden: Gothenburg University, 1979.

Wescott, Steven D. *A Comprehensive Bibliography of Music for Film and Television*. Detroit: Information Coordinators, 1985.

NEWS, DOCUMENTARY
AND PUBLIC AFFAIRS

Since 1963, more Americans have claimed to get most of their news from television than from any other source. Television news programs, documentaries, and public affairs provide information that viewers use to help form a "cognitive map" of their city, country, and world. Television news derives both its popularity and impact from its ability to visually re-present what appears to be reality and from its ability to present new information within a familiar format and ideological framework.

Early television network newscasts lasted only 15 minutes, but soon public affairs programming was added, including Edward R. Murrow's *See It Now*. In the 1960s, television news expanded in length at both the network and local station levels. Television news grew up as it covered major events such as the cold war, the Cuban missile crisis, the civil rights struggles, NASA space missions, the assassinations of President John Kennedy, Robert Kennedy, and Martin Luther King, Jr.; and the Vietnam War.

Television news, much like newspapers, functions in part as a watchdog on government. In 1969, when the Nixon administration felt their policy on the Vietnam War was being unfairly treated, Vice President Spiro Agnew gave a speech criticizing the small elite group of television executives who decide what will be on the news each night. Four years later, the commercial networks and public television broadcast live coverage of the Senate Watergate hearings and, one year later, Nixon's resignation speech.

In addition to newscasts, local and national television news organizations produce other types of programs, including interviews, documentaries, and public affairs. NBC's *Meet the Press* Sunday morning interview program is the longest running show on television. In the past, the commercial broadcast networks produced a greater number of documentaries; but today, in a quest of high ratings, the popular format is the hour-long "magazine" that typically features several segments (e.g., *Sixty Minutes*). PBS continues to offer *Frontline,* a series of independently-produced documentaries.

Today, television news can be a money-maker for local stations as well as for the networks. The pressure for high ratings, which translate into advertiser dollars, influences content. Over the years, local news has been especially criticized for "happy-talk" formats, superficiality, and sensationalism. A new phenomenon emerging in the 1980s was the syndicated program that offered a televised tabloid combination of information and entertainment or "infotainment." Focusing on the famous and the sensational, programs such as *Entertainment Tonight* and *A Current Affair* became popular and profitable.

Several technological developments helped change the nature of television news. When electronic news-gathering (ENG) replaced film, there was a quicker turn-around time between shooting the news and presenting it. Cable and satellite technologies allowed for live instantaneous transmission of news events from around the world as well as the emergence of the Cable News Network (CNN), the first 24-hour television news channel.

Many scholars have and continue to study television news from a variety of perspectives. For example, some researchers conduct content analyses of television news coverage of a particular issue or event. Others investigate the relationship between professional journalistic codes and news selection. Others debate ethical issues such as privacy and the relationship between confidentiality and the public interest. Still others offer evidence to support the critical argument that television news is far from objective because it confers status and legitimacy on certain individuals and groups at the expense of others.

Topic Suggestions

Biographical study of a current television journalist
C-SPAN
Cable News Network
Comparative analysis of commercial network and public television news
Comparative analysis of local television news coverage and newspaper
    treatment of same event
Comparative analysis of news coverage of Vietnam War and Persian Gulf
    War
Comparative analysis of television documentary and docudrama treatment
    of the same event
Cultural myths in television news

Economic analysis of news operations in major market television stations
Educating and training television journalists
Edward R. Murrow: television news pioneer
Ethical considerations in television news coverage of terrorist activities
Frontline (case study of a public television series featuring independently-
produced documentaries)
Gatekeeping: deciding what to include in a television newscast
"Happy Talk" and the evolution of local television news
HBO documentaries
Historical overview of commercial television network documentaries
History of public service announcements on television
How electronic newsgathering (ENG) changed television news
How television distorts the news
How television news influences public opinion
Infotainment (the merging of news and entertainment)
International cooperation in television newsgathering
Is there a liberal bias in television news?
Literature review of audience research related to television news
Naming rape victims: violation of privacy or public knowledge?
NBC Dateline fiasco (the faking of a fire in a GMC truck in a 1993 seg-
ment)
Satellite and microwave technology and their application in television news
Sixty Minutes: case study of a successful television news magazine pro-
gram
Sunday morning news interview and commentary programs
Tabloid news programs (e.g., *A Current Affair* and *Hard Copy*)
Television coverage of AIDS in public affairs programming
Television news coverage of environmental issues (case study of Three-Mile
Island nuclear accident)
Television news coverage of international affairs
Television news coverage of minorities
Television news coverage of social conflicts (e.g., race, gender, etc.)
Television news coverage of the 1990 Persian Gulf War (Operation Desert
Storm)
Use of video press releases in television news
Women on camera and behind the scenes in television news

Sources

Adams, William C. *Television Coverage of International Affairs*. Nor-
wood, NJ: Ablex, 1982.
Altheide, David. *Creating Reality: How TV News Distorts Events*. Beverly
Hills, Ca: Sage, 1986.
Arnett, Peter. *Live from the Battlefield: From Vietnam to Baghdad: 35
Years in the World's War Zones*. New York: Simon & Schuster, 1994.

Biagi, Shirley. *Newstalk II: State-of-the-Art Conversations with Today's Broadcast Journalists*. Belmont, CA: Wadsworth, 1987.

Bliss, Edward J. *Now the News: The Story of Broadcast Journalism*. New York: Columbia University Press, 1992.

Bluem, William A. *Documentary in American Television: Form, Function and Method*. New York: Hastings House, 1965.

Burns, Eric. *Broadcast Blues: Dispatches From the Twenty-Year War Between a Television Reporter and His Medium*. New York: Harper Collins, 1993.

Campbell, Richard. *60 Minutes and the News: A Mythology for Middle America*. Urbana: University of Illinois Press, 1991.

CBS News Television Broadcasts in Microform. (1975–). Ann Arbor, MI: University Microfilms International.

Coates, Charles. *Professional TV News Handbook*. Chicago: Bonus Books, 1994.

Cohen, Akiba A., Hanna Adoni and Charles R. Bantz. *Social Conflict and Television News*. Newbury Park, CA: Sage, 1990.

Cook, Philip S., Douglas Gomery and Lawrence W. Lichty, eds. *The Future of News: Television—Newspapers—Wire Services—Magazines*. Baltimore: Johns Hopkins University Press, 1991.

Cooper, Barry. *Sins of Omission: Shaping the News at CBC TV*. Toronto: University of Toronto Press, 1994.

Craft, Christine. *Too Old, Too Ugly & Not Deferential to Men: An Anchorwoman's Courageous Battle Against Sex Discrimination*. Rocklin, CA: Prima Publishing, 1988.

Diamond, Edwin. *The Media Show: The Changing Face of the News, 1985–1990*. Cambridge, MA: MIT Press, 1991.

Diamond, Edwin. *Sign Off: The Last Days of Television*. Cambridge, MA: MIT Press, 1982.

Dobkin, Bethami A. *Tales of Terror: Television News and the Construction of the Terrorist Threat*. Westport, CT: Praeger, 1992.

Donovan, Robert J. and Ray Scherer. *Unsilent Revolution: Television News and American Public Life, 1948–1991*. New York: Cambridge University Press, 1992.

Einstein, Daniel. *Special Edition: A Guide to Network Television Documentary Series and Special News Reports, 1955–1979*. Metuchen, NJ: Scarecrow Press, 1987.

Einstein, Daniel. *Special Edition: A Guide to Network Television Documentary Series and Special News Reports, 1980–1989*. Metuchen, NJ: Scarecrow Press, 1994.

Ellis, Jack C. *The Documentary Idea: A Critical History of English-Language Documentary Film and Video*. New York: Prentice-Hall, 1989.

Frank, Reuven. *Out of Thin Air: The Brief Wonderful Life of Network News*. New York: Simon & Schuster, 1991.

Gans, Herbert J. *Deciding What's News: A Study of CBS Evening News, NBC Nightly News, Newsweek, and Time*. New York: Pantheon, 1979.

Gitlin, Todd. *The Whole World is Watching: Mass Media in the Making and Unmaking of the New Left.* Berkeley, CA: University of California Press, 1980.
Glasgow University Media Group. *Bad News.* London: Routledge, 1976.
Goldberg, Robert and Gerald Jay Goldberg. *Anchors: Brokaw, Jennings, Rather and the Evening News.* New York: Birch Lane Press, 1990.
Goldman, Robert and Arvind Rajagopal, eds. *Mapping Hegemony: Television News & Industrial Conflict.* Norwood, NJ: Ablex, 1991.
Graham, Fred. *Happy Talk: Confessions of a TV Newsman.* New York: W.W. Norton, 1990.
Gunter, Barrie. *Poor Reception: Misunderstanding and Forgetting Broadcast News.* Hillsdale, NJ: Lawrence Erlbaum, 1987.
Gunther, Marc. *The House That Roone Built: The Inside Story of ABC News.* New York: Little Brown, 1994.
Hallin, Daniel. *The "Uncensored War": The Media and Vietnam.* New York: Oxford University Press, 1986.
Hallin, Daniel. *We Keep America on Top of the World: Television Journalism and the Public Sphere.* New York: Routledge, 1994.
Hammond, Charles Montgomery, Jr. *The Image Decade: Television Documentary 1965-1975.* New York: Hastings House, 1981.
Harrison, Martin. *TV News: Whose Bias? A Casebook Analysis of Strikes, Television and Media Studies.* Hermitage, Berkshire, England: Policy Journals, 1985.
Henson, Robert. *Television Weathercasting: A History.* Jefferson, NC: McFarland, 1990.
Hosley, David H. and Gayle K. Yamada. *Hard News: Women in Broadcast Journalism.* Westport, CT: Greenwood Press, 1987.
Iyengar, Shanto and Donald R. Kinder. *News That Matters: Television and American Opinion.* Chicago: University of Chicago Press, 1987.
Jacobs, Jerry. *Changing Channels: Issues and Realities in Television News.* Mountain View, CA: Mayfield Publishing, 1990.
James, Doug. *Walter Cronkite: His Life and Times.* Brentwood, TN: J.M. Press, 1991.
Joyce, Ed. *Prime Times, Bad Times.* New York: Anchor, 1989.
Keirstad, Phillip. *Modern Public Affairs Programming.* Blue Ridge Summit, PA: TAB Books, 1979.
Kellner, Douglas. *The Persian Gulf TV War.* Boulder, CO: Westview Press, 1992.
Larson, James F. *Television's Window on the World: International Affairs Coverage on the U.S. Networks.* Norwood, NJ: Ablex, 1985.
Lee, Martin A. and Norman Solomon. *Unreliable Sources: A Guide to Detecting Bias in News Media.* New York: Carol Publishing, 1990.
Lindekugel, D. M. *Shooters: TV News Photographers and Their Work.* Westport, CT: Greenwood Press, 1994.
MacKuen, Michael Bruce and Steven Lane Coombs. *More Than News: Media Power in Public Affairs.* Beverly Hills, CA: Sage, 1981.

Madsen, Axel. *Sixty Minutes: The Power and the Politics of America's Most Popular TV News Show*. New York: Dodd, Mead, and Company, 1984.

Matelski, Marilyn. *TV News Ethics*. Boston: Focal Press, 1991.

Musberger, Robert B. *Electronic News Gathering: A Guide to ENG*. Boston: Focal Press, 1991.

Nimmo, Dan and James E. Combs. *Nightly Horrors: Crisis Coverage by Television Network News*. Knoxville: University of Tennessee Press, 1985.

Oppenheimer, Jerry. *Barbara Walters: An Unauthorized Biography*. New York: St. Martin's Press, 1990.

Parenti, Michael. *Inventing Reality: The Politics of News Media*. 2nd ed. New York: St. Martin's Press, 1993.

Persico, Joseph E. *Edward R. Murrow: An American Original*. New York: McGraw-Hill, 1988.

Postman, Neil and Steve Powers. *How to Watch TV News*. New York: Penguin, 1992.

Powers, Ron. *The Newscasters: The News Business as Show Business*. Rev. ed. New York: St. Martin's Press, 1980.

Public Affairs Video Archives: The Education and Research Archives of C-SPAN Programming. (1987–present). West Lafayette, IN: Purdue University.

Reeves, Jimmie L. and Richard Campbell. *Cracked Coverage: Television News, the Anti-Cocaine Crusade, and the Reagan Legacy*. Durham, NC: Duke University Press, 1994.

Robinson, John P. and Mark R. Levy. *The Main Source: Learning from Television News*. Beverly Hills, CA: Sage, 1986.

Rosteck, Thomas. *See It Now Confronts McCarthyism: Television Documentary and the Politics of Representation*. Tuscaloosa: University of Alabama Press, 1994.

Schihl, Robert J. *TV Newscast Processes and Procedures*. Boston: Focal Press, 1991.

Smith, Myron J. Jr., comp. *U.S. Television Network News: A Guide to Sources in English*. Jefferson, NC: McFarland, 1984.

Steven, Peter. *Brink of Reality: New Canadian Documentary Film and Video*. Toronto: Between the Lines, 1993.

Stone, Vernon A. *Let's Talk Pay in Television and Radio News*. Chicago: Bonus Books, 1993.

Trotta, Liz. *Fighting for Air: In the Trenches with Television News*. New York: Simon & Schuster, 1991.

Westin, A.V. *Newswatch: How TV Decides the News*. New York: Simon & Schuster, 1982.

White, Ray. *TV News: Building a Career in Broadcast Journalism*. Stoneham, MA: Focal Press, 1989.

Whittemore, Hank. *CNN: The Inside Story*. New York: Little, Brown and Company, 1990.

Wiener, Robert. *Live From Baghdad: Gathering News at Ground Zero.* New York: Doubleday, 1992.

Wober, J. Mallory, ed. *Television and Nuclear Power: Making the Public Mind.* Norwood, NJ: Ablex, 1992.

Yoakam, Richard D. and Charles F. Cremer. *ENG: Television News and the New Technology.* 2nd ed. Carbondale: Southern Illinois University Press, 1989.

PERFORMANCE

This is a broad conceptual category because there are performance aspects to much of what we see on television. For purposes of discussion, we can break down this category into two basic parts — television performers and the performing arts on television.

Television performers include actors, announcers and narrators, talk and game show hosts, reporters and interviewers. The performer-audience relationship is a vital key to the success or failure of a television program. Performers must not only be able to successfully relate to viewers but must also work well with members of their production team as well as with fellow performers.

Performing on television is different than performing in other media. For example, television actors must use facial expressions to convey emotion much more than their theater counterparts. Television actors can re-shoot their lines if they goof, a luxury not afforded to actors on the live stage.

Today, the performing arts are featured on television on PBS and cable, such as the Bravo Network, via remote telecasts as well as in original productions made for the medium. The impact of television on the performing arts is debatable. No doubt, televised theater, opera, ballet, and classical music concerts have helped to expose millions of people to performing arts they might never had seen otherwise. However, some critics point out that television hurts local theater attendance and that televising theater denatures the aesthetic experience of the live performance.

(See also Comedy, Drama, Music)

Topic Suggestions

Announcing
Biography of a successful television actor (e.g., Larry Hagman)

74

Child actors on television
Comparative analysis of theatrical acting and television acting
Dance on television
Emmy awards: the television industry recognizes outstanding performances
Historical analysis of Hispanic television actors
History of television sports announcing
History of theatrical presentations on television
How to communicate effectively as interviewer or interviewee during a
    television interview
Impact of television on the performing arts
Influence of audience perception of news anchor performance on television
    ratings
PBS' *Great Performances* series
Performance programming on cable networks (e.g., Arts & Entertainment,
    and Bravo)
Performer-audience relationship
Screen tests and auditions
Television talk hosts: styles and techniques
Voice-overs for cartoon animation

Sources

Beardsley, Elaine K. *Working in Commercials: A Complete Sourcebook for
    Adult and Child Actors*. Boston: Focal Press, 1993.
Blum, Richard. *Working Actors: The Craft of Television, Film and Stage
    Performance*. Boston: Focal Press, 1989.
Blythin, Evan and Larry A. Samovar. *Communicating Effectively on Tele-
    vision*. Belmont, CA: Wadsworth, 1985.
Butler, Jeremy G., ed. *Star Texts: Image and Performance in Film and
    Television*. Detroit: Wayne State University Press, 1991.
*Contemporary Theatre, Film, and Television: A Biographical Guide
    Featuring Performers, Directors, Writers, Producers, Designers,
    Managers, Choreographers, Technicians, Composers, Executives,
    Dancers, and Critics in the United States and Great Britain*. 12
    volumes. Detroit: Gale Research, 1994.
Duerr, Edwin. *Radio & Television Acting: Criticism, Theory & Practice*.
    Westport, CT: Greenwood Press, 1972.
Earl Blackwell's Entertainment Celebrity Register. New York: Visible Ink
    Press, 1991.
Hawes, William. *Television Performing: News and Information*. Boston:
    Focal Press, 1991.
Keith, Michael C. *Broadcast Voice Performance*. Boston: Focal Press,
    1989.
Kliman, Bernice W. *Hamlet: Film, Television, and Audio Performance*.
    Rutherford, NJ: Fairleigh Dickinson University Press, 1980.

Kulzer, Dina-Marie. *Television Series Regulars of the Fifties and Sixties in Interview*. Jefferson, NC: McFarland, 1992.

O'Donnell, Lewis B., et al. *Announcing: Broadcast Communicating Today*. 2nd edition. Belmont, CA: Wadsworth, 1992.

O'Neill, Thomas. *Emmys: Star Wars, Showdowns, and the Supreme Test of TV's Best*. New York: Penguin, 1992.

Paietta, Ann. *Animals on Screen and Radio: An Annotated Sourcebook*. Metuchen, NJ: Scarecrow Press, 1994.

Parish, James R. and Vincent Terrace. *The Complete Actors' Television Credits, 1948–1988*. 2nd ed. 2 vol. Metuchen, NJ: Scarecrow Press, 1989–90.

Rose, Brian. *Television and the Performing Arts*. Westport, CT: Greenwood Press, 1986.

Rose, Brian. *Televising the Performing Arts: Interviews with Merrill Brockway, Kirk Browning, and Roger Englander*. Westport, CT: Greenwood Press, 1992.

Tucker, Patrick. *How to Act for the Camera*. New York: Routledge, 1993.

Ward, Jack. *Television Guest Stars: An Illustrated Career Chronicle for 678 Performers of the Sixties and Seventies*. Jefferson, NC: McFarland, 1993.

POLITICS

Television plays a vital role in politics and political socialization in the United States. Politics on television takes many forms — campaign advertising, debates, election coverage, news, press conferences, speeches, C-SPAN, and so on. Whatever the form, the role of television in the American political process, similar to the printed press, continues to be that of the "fourth estate" in a democratic society, acting as both a communications channel and a public watchdog over our three branches of government — executive, legislative, and judicial.

Much of the published research on television and politics focuses on the executive branch of the federal government, especially on presidential affairs. From the historical viewpoint, there are several studies from President Eisenhower to the present administration as to how individual administrations have attempted to use television for political purposes. Although there is little research to suggest that television significantly influences voting behavior, the medium has contributed to other profound structural changes in the American political system of nominating and electing presidents. For example, political consultants and public opinion pollsters have replaced political party bosses by marketing candidates directly to the public via mass media, particularly television.

An important area of research concerning the relationship of television and politics is the role and impact of television news journalists on public opinion of politicians and political issues. Television news agenda-setting, the issues and events chosen for presentation, may have considerable influence on public opinion, such as when journalists report on the private lives of public politicians. Also significant is how television news covers domestic and foreign policy issues, the public opinion that is influenced by such coverage, and then how politicians react to the public opinion.

(See also International, News, Regulation and Policy)

Topic Suggestions

C-SPAN programming

Cable News Network (CNN) and its influence on foreign policy opinion
leaders and politicians

Celebrities as special interest spokespersons and political opinion leaders

Comparative analysis of how different U.S. presidents have used television

Comparative analysis of print and television coverage of a political issue or
political campaign

Comparative analysis of the relationship between politics and television in
the United States and in one or more other countries

Effects of television coverage on presidential campaigns

Effects of television coverage on public perception of candidates and issues

Electronic town meetings (television and political participation)

Historical relationship between television and a significant political figure

History and influence of televised political debates, beginning with the
famous Kennedy-Nixon debates

History of *Meet the Press* and other political interview and commentary
programming

History of political advertising on television

Influence of television news on political agenda-setting

Influence of television news on public opinion concerning political issues

News coverage of the Cold War

Political ideology in television drama and/or comedy

Politics as entertainment

The politics of television regulation

Politics on public television

Positive vs. negative political advertising

Regulation: Section 315 of the Communications Act and politics on television

Reporting about the private lives of public politicians

Role of television journalists in covering elections

Teledemocracy and citizenship

Televised Senate hearings (e.g., Watergate, Iran-Contra, Clarence Thomas)

Television and political campaign reform

Television and presidential press conferences

Television news coverage of political polls

U.S. foreign policy, national security, and television

Uses of television by religious and special interest organizations to influence
the political agenda

Vietnam: politics and television at war

Sources

Abramson, Jeffrey B. and others. *The Electronic Commonwealth: The Impact of New Media Technologies on Democratic Politics.* New York:
Basic Books, 1988.

Adams, William C., ed. *Television Coverage of the 1980 Presidential Campaign*. Norwood, NJ: Ablex, 1983.

Allen, Craig. *Eisenhower and the Mass Media: Peace, Prosperity, and Prime-Time TV*. Chapel Hill: University of North Carolina Press, 1993.

Altheide, David L. "The Impact of Television News Formats on Social Policy." *Journal of Broadcasting and Electronic Media* 35 (Winter 1991): 3-21.

Barkin, Steven M. "Eisenhower's Television Planning Board: An Unwritten Chapter in the History of Political Broadcasting." *Journal of Broadcasting* 27 (Fall 1983): 319-331.

Biocca, Frank, ed. *Television and Political Advertising*. Hillsdale, NJ: Lawrence Erlbaum Associates, 1991.

Blume, Keith. *The Presidential Election Show: Campaign 84 and Beyond on the Nightly News*. South Hadley, MA: Bergin & Garvey, 1985.

Blumler, Jay G. and Dennis McQuail. *Television in Politics: Its Uses and Influence*. Chicago: University of Chicago Press, 1969.

Brownstein, Ronald. *The Power and the Glitter: The Hollywood-Washington Connection*. New York: Pantheon, 1990.

Diamond, Edwin and Stephen Bates. *The Spot: The Rise of Political Advertising on Television*. 3rd ed. Cambridge, MA: MIT Press, 1992.

Dover, E. D. *Presidential Elections in the Television Age*. Westport, CT: Greenwood Press, 1994.

Franklin, Bob, ed. *Televising Democracies*. New York: Routledge, 1992.

Garay, Ronald. *Congressional Television: A Legislative History*. Westport, CT: Greenwood Press, 1984.

Gitlin, Todd. "Blips, Bites, and Savvy Talk: Television's Impact on American Politics." *Dissent* 37 (Winter 1990): 18-26.

Graber, Doris A. *Media Power in Politics*. 2nd ed. Washington, DC: Congressional Quarterly Press, 1990.

Hallin, Daniel C. "Sound Bite News: Television Coverage of Elections, 1968-1988." *Journal of Communication* 42 (Spring 1992): 5-24.

Hellweg, Susan A., Michael Pfau and Steven R. Bryden. *Televised Presidential Debates: Advocacy in Contemporary America*. New York: Praeger, 1992.

Iyengar, Shanto. *Is Anyone Responsible?: How Television Frames Political Issues*. Chicago: University of Chicago Press, 1991.

Jamieson, Kathleen Hall. *Packaging the Presidency: A History and Criticism of Presidential Campaign Advertising*. 2nd ed. New York: Oxford University Press, 1992.

Kaid, Lynda Lee and Anne Johnston. "Negative Versus Positive Television Advertising in the U.S. Presidential Campaigns, 1960-1988." *Journal of Communication* 41 (Summer 1991): 53-64.

Kaid, Lynda Lee and Anne Johnston Wadsworth. *Political Campaign Communication: A Bibliography and Guide to the Literature 1973-1982*. Metuchen, NJ: Scarecrow, 1985.

Kaid, Lynda Lee and Kathleen J.M. Haynes. *Political Commercial Archive: A Catalog and Guide to the Collection*. Norman: University of Oklahoma, Political Communication Center, 1991.

Kellner, Douglas. *Television and the Crisis of Democracy*. Boulder, CO: Westview Press, 1990.

Kerbel, Matthew R. *Edited for Television: CNN, ABC, and the 1992 Presidential Campaign*. Boulder, CO: Westview Press, 1994.

Kern, Montague. *30-Second Politics: Political Advertising in the Eighties*. New York: Praeger, 1989.

King, Larry with Mark Stencel. *On the Line: The New Road to the White House*. New York: Harcourt Brace & Company, 1993.

Lang, Gladys E. and Kurt Lang. *Politics and Television: Reviewed*. Beverly Hills: Sage, 1984.

MacDonald, J. Fred. *Television and the Red Menace: The Video Road to Vietnam*. New York: Praeger, 1985.

Mazzoco, Dennis W. *Networks of Power: Corporate TV's Threat to Democracy*. Boston: South End Press, 1994.

Mickelson, Sig. *From Whistle Stop to Sound Bite: Four Decades of Politics and Television*. New York: Praeger, 1989.

Mickiewicz, Ellen and Charles Firestone. *Television & Elections*. Queenstown, MD.: Aspen Institute and Carter Center of Emory University, 1992.

Nimmo, Dan and James E. Combs. *Mediated Political Realities*. 2nd ed. Longman, 1990.

O'Neill, Michael J. *The Roar of the Crowd: How Television and People Power Are Changing the World*. New York: Times Books, 1993.

Ranney, Austin. *Channels of Power: The Impact of Television on American Politics*. New York: Basic Books, 1983.

Rosenstiel, Tom. *Strange Bedfellows: How Television and the Presidential Candidates Changed American Politics, 1992*. New York: Hyperion, 1993.

Schram, Martin. *The Great American Video Game: Presidential Politics in the Television Age*. New York: Wm. Morrow, 1987.

Smoller, Frederic T. *The Six O'Clock Presidency: A Theory of Presidential Press Relations in the Age of Television*. Westport, CT: Praeger, 1990.

Stempel, Guido H. III. and John W. Windhauser, eds. *The Media in the 1984 and 1988 Presidential Campaigns*. Westport, CT: Greenwood Press, 1991.

Swerdlow, Joel. L. *Presidential Debates: 1988 and Beyond*. Washington, DC: CQ Press, 1987.

Tannenbaum, Percy H. and Leslie Kostrich. *Turned-On TV/Turned-Off Voters: Policy Options for Election Projections*. Beverly Hills, CA: Sage, 1983.

Twentieth Century Fund. *With the Nation Watching: Report of the Twentieth Century Fund Task Force on Televised Presidential Debates*. New York: Lexington Books, 1979.

West, Darrell M. *Air Wars: Television Advertising in Election Campaigns, 1952-1992*. Washington, D.C.: Congressional Quarterly, 1993.

PRODUCTION

The United States produces more hours of television programming annually than any other country. The majority of all production is done by networks and independent producers based in Los Angeles and New York. Most productions are recorded for later broadcast or cablecast, but some programming is produced live, including sporting events, award shows, and the news.

Most television productions can be broken down into three distinct phases. The first phase, pre-production, refers to all the work necessary before the actual shooting begins, such as budgeting, casting, obtaining insurance, and so on. The second phase is the actual production, which takes place in a television studio and/or on location. The third phase is post-production, which includes editing and other work needed to finish the project.

The budgets for television productions are normally broken down into above-the-line and below-the-line costs. Above-the-line refers largely to the costs of the writers, cast, producers, and director; while below-the-line refers to most other expenses, including technical crew, sets, costumes, props, catering services for on-location shooting, and so on.

In television production, executive producers hire producers and directors to help them create their programming products. There has been usually a handful of very successful executive producers at any given time throughout the history of television. For example, in the 1970s, Garry Marshall produced several situation comedies, including *The Odd Couple, Mork and Mindy, Happy Days,* and *Laverne and Shirley.*

Television directors are responsible for shooting the scripts. Directors give their productions a style by manipulating several production variables, including camera distance, movement, and angles; lighting, and sound. Television production styles can range from creating the illusion of reality to creating expressionistic video art.

(See also Programming)

Topic Suggestions

Aesthetic analysis of the use of the hand-held camera in television drama

Challenges of producing television programs on location

Comparative analysis of advantages and disadvantages of on-location and television studio production

Comparative analysis of lighting techniques in two or more television programs

Comparative analysis of live and taped television production of a cultural performance

Comparative analysis of special effects and editing styles in car commercials produced in each of the last four decades

Comparative analysis of television production budgets for various types of programming

Computer graphics, chroma key, and more: producing the weather segment for the local television newscast

Critical analysis of the television work of a prolific television producer (e.g., Steve Bochco or Stephen Cannell)

Directorial styles in television dramas

Economic analysis of doing television production in Canada instead of in the United States

Economic analysis of television network news production

Historical analysis of television's best writers

History of television animation production techniques

History of television special effects

How to produce effective television programming for children

How will high-definition television (HDTV) affect production styles and techniques?

Live sports production

Pre-production: a case study of the Super Bowl

Putting it all together: how still photographs, voices, music, and sound effects were combined in the making of Ken Burns' *The Civil War* series on PBS

Set designs for new programs

Sound effects in advertising and their impact on viewer attention

Television production and the labor unions: a case study of the National Association of Broadcast Electrical Technicians (NABET)

Sources

Anderson, Gary. H. *Video Editing and Post-Production: A Professional Guide.* 2nd ed. White Plains, NY: Knowledge Industry Publications, 1988.

Armer, Alan A. *Writing the Screenplay: TV & Film*. 2nd ed. Belmont, CA: Wadsworth, 1993.

Barker, David. "Television Production Techniques as Communication," in *Television: The Critical View*. 5th ed. Edited by Horace Newcomb. New York: Oxford University Press, 1994.

Blum, Richard and Richard D. Lindheim. *Inside Television Producing*. Boston: Focal Press, 1991.

Blumenthal, Howard J. *Television Producing and Directing*. New York: Harper & Row, 1987.

Brady, Ben. *Principles of Adaptation for Film and Television*. Austin: University of Texas Press, 1994.

Breyer, Richard and Peter Moller. *Making Television Programs: A Professional Approach*. Prospect Heights, IL: Waveland Press, 1991.

Brown, Blain. *Motion Picture and Video Lighting*. Boston: Focal Press, 1992.

Burrows, Thomas D., Donald N. Wood and Lynne Schafer Gross. *Television Production: Disciplines & Techniques*. 5th ed. Dubuque, IA: Wm. C. Brown, 1992.

Cantor, Muriel G. *The Hollywood TV Producer: His Work and His Audience*. New York: Transaction, 1987.

Clifford, Martin. *Microphones*. 3rd ed. Blue Ridge Summit, PA: TAB Books, 1986.

Colby, Lewis and Tom Greer. *The TV Director-Interpreter*. Rev. ed. New York: Hastings, 1990.

Compesi, Ronald J. and Ronald E. Sherriffs. *Video Field Production and Editing. 3rd ed*. Boston: Allyn and Bacon, 1994.

Fielding, Ken. *Introduction to Television Production*. New York: Longman, 1990.

Fitt, Brian and Joe Thornley. *The Control of Light*. Boston: Focal Press, 1992.

Grant, Eustace. *Writing for Corporate Videos*. Boston: Focal Press, 1990.

Gregg, Rodman W., ed. *Who's Who in Television: Writers, Directors, Producers and the Networks*. Beverly Hills: Packard, 1987.

Huber, David Miles. *Audio Production Techniques for Video*. Indianapolis, IN: Howard W. Sams, 1987.

Jarvis, Peter. *A Production Handbook: A Practical Guide to the Pitfalls of Programme Making*. Boston: Focal Press, 1993.

Johnston, Carla B. *International Television Co-Production from Access to Success*. Boston: Focal Press, 1992.

Kehoe, Vincent J. R. *The Technique of the Professional Make-Up Artist for Film, Television, and Stage*. Boston: Focal Press, 1985.

Kuney, Jack. *Take One: Television Directors on Directing*. Westport, CT: Greenwood Press, 1990.

Levinson, Richard and William Link. *Off Camera: Conversations with the Makers of Prime-Time Television*. New York: New American Library, 1986.

Lindheim, Richard D. and Richard A. Blum. *Inside Television Producing.* Boston: Focal Press, 1991.

Millerson, Gerald. *The Technique of Lighting for Television and Film.* 3rd ed. Boston: Focal Press, 1991.

Millerson, Gerald. *TV Scenic Design Handbook.* Boston: Focal Press, 1989.

Millerson, Gerald. *Video Camera Techniques.* 2nd ed. Boston: Focal Press, 1994.

Mott, Robert L. *Sound Effects: Radio, TV, and Film.* Boston: Focal Press, 1990.

Naylor, Lynne, ed. *Television Directors Guide.* Beverly Hills: Lone Eagle, 1991.

Newcomb, Horace and Robert S. Alley, eds. *The Producer's Medium: Conversations with Creators of American TV.* New York: Oxford University Press, 1983.

Oringel, Robert S. *Audio Control Handbook for Radio and Television Broadcasting.* 6th ed. Boston: Focal Press, 1989.

Schihl, Robert. *Single Camera Video: From Concept to Edited Master.* Boston: Focal Press, 1989.

Smith, David L. *Video Communication: Structuring Content for Maximum Programming Effectiveness.* Belmont, CA: Wadsworth, 1991.

Stempel, Tom. *Storytellers to the Nation: A History of American Television Writing.* New York: Continuum, 1992.

Thompson, Robert J. and Gary Burns, eds. *Making Television: Authorship and the Production Process.* Westport, CT: Praeger, 1990.

Verna, Tony and William Bode. *Live TV: An Inside Look at Directing and Producing.* Boston: Focal Press, 1987.

White, Hooper. *How to Produce Effective TV Commercials.* 3rd ed. Lincolnwood, IL: NTC Publishing, 1994.

Wiegand, Ingrid and Ben Bogossian. *Professional Video Production.* 2nd ed. White Plains, NY: Knowledge Industry Publications, 1993.

Wilkie, Bernard. *The Technique of Special Effects in Television.* 2nd ed. London: Focal Press, 1989.

Zettl, Herbert. *Television Production Handbook.* 5th ed. Belmont, CA: Wadsworth, 1992.

PROGRAMMING

Since the 1970s, due to the proliferation of cable and other newer technologies, scores of new television channels have been created, and there has been a consequent increase in the volume and diversity of television programs. Today, for example, there are all-news, sports, weather, movies, cartoons, comedy, court, and shopping cable programming services.

Television stations and networks are in the business of providing programming to viewers. Stations and networks produce their own programming and/or acquire the right to show programs produced by others. Most programming in the United States is aimed at attracting large audiences that will also be attractive to advertisers. (Many television programs in the early days of the medium were produced by the sponsors themselves.) Stations and networks compete for large audiences by employing a variety of programming strategies, such as "sandwiching," the strategy of scheduling a new program between two established hit programs.

Noncommercial programming, such as that on PBS and C-SPAN, provides alternatives to a largely commercial television landscape. Premium pay-cable services, such as HBO, and pay-per-view also offer commercial-free programs.

The various types or genres of television programming have different origins. For example, the western, drama, and science fiction genres were largely influenced by cinematic style. Other programming, particularly soap operas and situation comedies, migrated to television from radio. Still other programming is unique to the medium, such as the infomercial. Genres are mutable, and new hybrids (e.g., the docudrama and the dramedy) have evolved over time. The cost of programming varies by genre. For example, daytime programming, including game shows and talk shows, tends to be less expensive to produce than prime time programming, such as the action-adventure series.

U.S. television programming is popular around the world and constitutes one of this country's major cultural exports. In addition to exhibiting U.S. programming, several countries also produce their own shows based upon the U.S. format (e.g., *Sesame Street* and *Wheel of Fortune*).

(See also Comedy, Drama, News, Public Television, Religion, Sports)

Topic Suggestions

Advertiser influence on television programming
Alternative programming in the United States
Appeal of various program genres to specific demographic groups
Auteur analysis of television programs of a prolific writer, producer, or
    director (e.g., producer Aaron Spelling)
Broadcast standards and practices: the networks' influence on television
    program content
The business of exporting U.S. television programs to foreign markets
Comparative analysis of audiences and programming strategies for daytime
    and prime time television
Comparative analysis of the volume and type of television programs
    available in the United States with that in one or more other countries
Court TV
Economic analysis of television program production by genre
The economics of narrowcasting or *niche programming*
The future impact of public affairs programming in a 500-channel television
    universe
Game shows and the celebration of merchandising
Genre analysis of news and information programming
Historical analysis of a long-running television program (e.g., *Meet the
    Press*)
Historical analysis of late-night television programming
Historical analysis of one or more television program genres
Home shopping programs
How a program gets on television
How television program syndication works
How TBS programs its broadcast and cable properties (WTBS, CNN, CNN
    Headline News, TNT, and the Cartoon Network)
Literature review of content analysis studies of violence in television pro-
    grams
Network programming strategies
Non-commercial programming in the United States
Non-English television programming in the United States
Programming the upcoming 500-channel universe
Social-psychological analysis of television program preferences by gender

Sports programming strategies
Star Trek: a case study of the transition of a television program to a motion
    picture and back again
Talk shows as a form of "tele-participatory" discourse
Telethons
Television program guides for viewers (including *TV Guide*): past, present,
    and future
Television program spin-offs as a programming strategy
Uses and gratifications of game show viewers
The utilization of talk shows by candidates in the 1992 Presidential election
Who owns the television programs you watch?

Sources

Adler, Richard, ed. *All in the Family: A Critical Appraisal*. New York:
    Praeger, 1979.
Anderson, Kent. *Television Fraud: The History and Implications of the
    Quiz Show Scandals*. Westport, CT: Greenwood Press, 1978.
Bailey, Robert Lee. *An Examination of Prime Time Network Television
    Special Programs, 1948–1966*. New York: Arno, 1979.
Baughman, James L. *Television's Guardians: The FCC and the Politics of
    Programming 1958–1967*. Knoxville: The University of Tennessee
    Press, 1985.
Blum Richard A. and Richard D. Lindheim. *Primetime: Network Televi-
    sion Programming*. Boston: Focal Press, 1987.
Boddy, William. "Alternative Television in the United States," in *Televi-
    sion: The Critical View*. 5th ed. Edited by Horace Newcomb. New
    York: Oxford University Press, 1994.
Bowles, Jerry. *A Thousand Sundays: The Story of The Ed Sullivan Show*.
    New York: Putnam, 1980.
Cantor, Muriel G. and Joel M. Cantor. *Prime-Time Television: Content
    and Control*. 2nd ed. Newbury Park, CA: Sage, 1992.
Carbaugh, Donal. *Talking American: Cultural Discourses on Donahue*.
    Norwood, NJ: Ablex, 1989.
Carroll. Raymond L. and Donald M. Davis. *Electronic Media Program-
    ming: Strategies and Decision Making*. New York: McGraw-Hill, 1993.
Carter, Bill. *The Late Shift: Letterman, Leno, and the Network Battle for
    the Night*. New York: Hyperion, 1994.
Castleman, Harry and Walter J. Podrazik. *The TV Schedule Book: Four
    Decades of Network Programming from Sign-On to Sign-Off*. New
    York: McGraw-Hill, 1984.
Conquest, John. *Trouble Is Their Business: Private Eyes in Fiction, Film,
    and Television, 1927–1988*. New York: Garland, 1990.
DeLong, Thomas A. *Quiz Craze: America's Infatuation with the Radio &
    Television Game Shows*. Westport, CT: Greenwood Press, 1991.

Eastman, Susan Tyler. *Broadcast/Cable Programming: Strategies and Practices*. 4th ed. Belmont, CA: Wadsworth Publishing, 1993.

Gerani, Gary and Paul H. Schulman. *Fantastic Television: A Pictorial History of Sci-Fi, the Unusual and Fantastic from Captain Video to the Star Trek Phenomenon and Beyond*. New York: Harmony Books, 1977.

Gianakos, Larry J. *Television Drama Series Programming*. 5 vols. Metuchen, NJ: Scarecrow Press, 1978–1987.

Gibberman, Susan R. *Star Trek*. Jefferson, NC: McFarland, 1991.

Godfrey, Donald G., compiler. *Reruns on File: A Guide to Electronic Media Archives*. Hillsdale, NJ: Lawrence Erlbaum Associates, 1992.

Goldberg, Lee. *Television Series Revivals: Sequels or Remakes of Cancelled Shows*. Jefferson, NC: McFarland, 1993.

Goldberg, Lee. *Unsold Television Pilots, 1955–1989*. Jefferson, NC: McFarland, 1990.

Holbrook, Morris B. *Daytime Television Game Shows and the Celebration of Merchandise: The Price Is Right*. Bowling Green, OH: Bowling Green State University Popular Press, 1993.

Howard, Herbert, Michael Kievman and Barbara Moore. *Radio, TV, and Cable Programming*. 2nd ed. Ames: Iowa State University Press, 1994.

Kaminsky, Stuart M. and Jeffrey H. Mahan. *American Television Genres*. Chicago: Nelson-Hall, 1985.

Lance, Steven. *Written Out of Television: The Encyclopedia of Cast Changes and Character Replacements 1945–Present*. Metuchen, NJ: Scarecrow Press, 1994.

Larka, Robert. *Television's Private Eye: An Examination of Twenty Years of Programming of a Particular Genre, 1949–1969*. New York: Arno, 1973.

Lenburg, Jeff. *The Encyclopedia of Animated Cartoons*. New York: Facts on File, 1991.

Livingstone, Sonia and Peter Lunt. *Talk on Television: Audience Participation and Public Debate*. New York: Routledge, 1994.

McNeil, Alex. *Total Television: A Comprehensive Guide to Programming from 1948 to the Present*. Updated 3rd ed. New York: Penguin, 1994.

Marc, David and Robert J. Thompson. *Prime Time, Prime Movers: From I Love Lucy to L.A. Law — America's Greatest TV Shows and the People Who Created Them*. Boston: Little, Brown, 1992.

Martindale, David. *Television Detective Shows of the 1970s*. Jefferson, NC: McFarland, 1991.

Matelski, Marilyn J. *Daytime Television Programming*. Stoneham, MA: Focal Press, 1991.

National Endowment for the Arts. *The Arts on Television, 1976–1990: Fifteen Years of Cultural Programming supported by the National Endowment for the Arts*. Washington, DC: National Endowment for the Arts, 1992.

Noam, Eli M. and Joel C. Millonzi, eds. *The International Market in Film and Television Programs*. Norwood, NJ: Ablex, 1993.

O'Neil, Thomas. *The Emmys: Star Wars, Showdowns, and the Supreme Test of TV's Best*. New York: Penguin Books, 1992.

Paisner, Daniel. *Horizontal Hold: The Making and Breaking of a Network Pilot*. New York: Birch Lane Press, 1992.

Prouty, Howard H., ed. *Variety Television Reviews, 1923–1988*. New York: Garland Publishing, 1989.

Rose, Brian G. *Television and the Performing Arts: A Handbook and Reference Guide to American Cultural Programming*. Westport, CT: Greenwood Press, 1986.

Rose, Brian G., ed. *TV Genres: A Handbook and Reference Guide*. Westport, CT: Greenwood Press, 1985.

Sackett, Susan. *Prime-Time Hits: Television's Most Popular Network Programs*. New York: Billboard Books, 1993.

Sams, David R. and Robert L. Shook. *Wheel of Fortune*. New York: St. Martin's Press, 1987.

Schihl, Robert. *Talk Show & Entertainment Program Processes & Procedures*. Boston: Focal Press, 1991.

Schwartz, David and others. *The Encyclopedia of TV Game Shows*. New York: New York Zoetrope, 1987.

Shapiro, Mitchell E. *Television Network Daytime and Late-Night Programming, 1959–1989*. Jefferson, NC: McFarland, 1990.

Shatner, William with Chris Kreski. *Star Trek Memories*. New York: HarperCollins, 1993.

Terrace, Vincent. *Encyclopedia of Television Series, Pilots and Specials*. 3 vols. New York: New York Zoetrope, 1985, 1986.

Terrace, Vincent. *Fifty Years of Television: A Guide to Series and Pilots, 1937–1988*. New York: Cornwall, 1991.

Terrace, Vincent. *Television Character and Story Facts: 1,008 Shows, 1945–1992*. Jefferson, NC: McFarland, 1993.

Terrace, Vincent. *Television Specials: 3,197 Entertainment Spectaculars, 1939 Through 1992*. Jefferson, NC: McFarland, 1994.

Thompson, Robert J. *Adventures on Prime Time: The Television Programs of Stephen J. Cannell*. Westport, CT: Praeger, 1990.

Tuchman, Gaye. *The TV Establishment: Programming for Power and Profit*. Englewood Cliffs, NJ: Prentice Hall, 1974.

West, Richard. *Television Westerns: Major and Minor Series, 1946–1978*. Jefferson, NC: McFarland, 1987.

Woolery, George W. *Animated TV Specials: The Complete Directory to the First Twenty-Five Years, 1962–1987*. Metuchen, NJ: Scarecrow Press, 1989.

PSYCHOLOGICAL
ASPECTS

Much television research has concerned psychological aspects of the relationship between individuals and the medium. It is fair to say that the research suggests that television can have both positive and negative influences on individuals. For example, on the positive side, television can play a beneficial therapeutic role during the rehabilitation process in the treatment of some childhood illnesses. However, the popular perception is that television has a largely negative psychological impact, such as desensitizing viewers to violent behavior.

In fact, a popular subject of academic study has been television's effect on behavior. Experiments suggest that television can serve as an agent for attitudinal and behavioral learning, formation, reinforcement, and change. One of the drawbacks of most of this research is that it concerns only short-term behavioral effects measured immediately or relatively shortly after the viewing experience. Long-term psychological effects of television are much more difficult to measure because it is almost impossible to single out television as the dominant variable in influencing certain behaviors.

Another area of psychological research focuses on television and cognitive development. This research orientation is concerned with how different individuals, especially children, comprehend and learn from television. Observational learning theory suggests that behavior on television serves as a model that can be learned by viewers. According to this psychological theory, individuals internalize observed televised behaviors into their own cognitive frameworks. In this sense, television can influence attitudes and perceptions about everyday life as well as behavior. Ultimately, of course, it is difficult to generalize about the psychological influence of television because individuals are unique and bring diverse attitudes, genetic dispositions, and cognitive abilities to their viewing experiences.

(See also Audience, Children, Criticism & Theory, Social Aspects)

Topic Suggestions

The American Psychological Association and the history of its positions
toward television
Applications of video and television in psychological therapy
Cognitive developmental considerations in producing programming for
young children
Depiction of the professional fields of psychology and psychiatry in enter-
tainment programming
Freudian or Jungian analysis of a television program
Individual differences in television comprehension
Information processing and learning from television
Is there such a thing as television addiction?
Loneliness and television use
Psychological analysis of the "television personality"
Psychological predictors of television viewing motivation
Psychological theories concerning the consequences of viewing aggressive
behavior on television
Psychologists on television (e.g., Dr. Joyce Brothers and Dr. Ruth West-
heimer)
Review of the literature on the psychological uses and gratifications of
television viewing
Television and catharsis
Television and its relation to fantasy and/or dreaming
Television and sexual learning in teenagers
Television and viewer apathy and/or withdrawal
Television and viewer role-modeling behavior
Television and self-concept among minority groups
What types of attitudes and behaviors might be influenced by television?

Sources

Baggaley, J., M. Ferguson and P. Brooks. *Psychology of the TV Image*.
New York: Praeger, 1980.
Ball-Rokeach, Sandra, Milton Rokeach and Joel W. Grube. *The Great
American Values Test: Influencing Behavior and Belief Through Tele-
vision*. New York: Free Press, 1984.
Bryant, Jennings and Dolf Zillmann, eds. *Media Effects: Advances in
Theory and Research*. Hillsdale, NJ: Lawrence Erlbaum Associates,
1994.
Bryant, Jennings and Dolf Zillmann. *Responding to the Screen: Reception
and Reaction Processes*. Hillsdale, NJ: Lawrence Erlbaum Associates,
1991.

Comstock, George, et al. *Television and Human Behavior*. New York: Columbia University Press, 1978.

Condry, John. *The Psychology of TV*. Hillsdale, NJ: Lawrence Erlbaum, 1989.

Fryrear, G. and B. Fleshman, eds. *Videotherapy in Mental Health*. Springfield, IL: C. C. Thomas Publishers, 1991.

Greenfield, Patricia Marks. *Mind and Media: The Effects of Television, Video Games, and Computers*. Cambridge, MA: Harvard University Press, 1984.

Gunter, B. *TV and the Fear of Crime*. London: John Libbey, 1987.

Huston, Aletha C., et al. *Big World, Small Screen: The Role of Television in American Society*. Lincoln: University of Nebraska Press, 1992.

Kubey, Robert and Mihaly Csikszentmihalyi. *Television and the Quality of Life: How Viewing Shapes Everyday Experience*. Hillsdale, NJ: Lawrence Erlbaum Associates, 1990.

Lang, Annie, ed. *Measuring Psychological Responses to Media Messages*. Hillsdale, NJ: Lawrence Erlbaum Associates, 1994.

Livingstone, Sonia. *Making Sense of Television: The Psychology of Audience Interpretation*. New York: Pergamon Books, 1990.

Milgram, Stanley and R. Lance Shotland. *Television and Antisocial Behavior*. New York: Academic Press, 1973.

Neuman, W. Russell. "The Psychology of the New Media," in *Television for the 21st Century: The Next Wave*. Edited by Charles M. Firestone. Washington, D.C.: The Aspen Institute, 1993.

Perse, Elizabeth M. and Alan M. Rubin. "Chronic Loneliness and Television Use." *Journal of Broadcasting & Electronic Media* (Winter 1990): 37–53.

Television and Behavior: Ten Years of Scientific Progress and Implications. 2 vols. Washington, DC: Government Printing Office, 1982.

Van Evra, Judith. *Television and Child Development*. Hillsdale, NJ: Lawrence Erlbaum Associates, 1990.

White, Mimi. *Tele-advising: Therapeutic Discourse in American Television*. Chapel Hill: University of North Carolina Press, 1992.

Wober, Joseph M. *The Use & Abuse of Television: A Social Psychological Analysis of the Changing Screen*. Hillsdale, NJ: Lawrence Erlbaum Associates, 1988.

PUBLIC TELEVISION

Today, public television in the United States plays a significant role in a largely profit-driven television environment. From its beginnings, television has been predominantly a commercial medium. However, also in the early years, there was public pressure for noncommercial educational broadcasting. In the 1950s, the Federal Communications Commission authorized the reservation of 242 noncommercial channels, mostly on the UHF band. In 1953, KUHT at the University of Houston became the first licensed educational channel. Due to the high cost of starting a television operation, few educational stations went on the air compared to their commercial counterparts. The early educational stations received financial assistance for facilities and programming from the Ford Foundation.

In 1967, the Carnegie Foundation's Commission on Educational Television changed the term from "educational" to "public" television and recommended a well-funded, pervasive broadcasting system to meet the needs of the American public. Many of the Carnegie Commission's recommendations became part of the Public Broadcasting Act of 1967, which created the Corporation for Public Broadcasting (CPB), and led to the formation of the Public Broadcasting Service (PBS).

Public television began offering alternative programming to that of the commercial networks. Early popular programs included *Sesame Street*, *The French Chef*, *Black Journal*, and *Washington Week in Review*. Imported cultural programming, such as the *Civilisation* series from Great Britain, was critically praised. However, public television has never been without its critics. During the Nixon administration, for example, CPB funding was cut because conservatives claimed a liberal, anti-administration bias in its programming.

In fact, one of the ongoing problems with public television is lack of adequate funding. Today, most public television stations are licensed to one of four entities: a state government commission, public school system, university, or community nonprofit corporation. Station and program funding today comes from a variety of sources, including Congress, state and local governments, corporate underwriting, viewer memberships, television auctions, and other special fundraising events.

The future of public television is uncertain. Cable television, while providing viewers better access to public television channels (especially those on the UHF band), also duplicates some of public television's programming. Some politicians have called for an end to government support of public television. This seems unlikely, as PBS continues to find ways of using new telecommunications technologies to reach new constituencies (e.g., the Adult Learning Service, and special services for the seeing and hearing impaired.)

(See also Education)

Topic Suggestions

Before PBS: The Ford Foundation and National Educational Television (NET)
Carnegie Commission for Educational Television (how their recommendations led to the Public Broadcasting Act of 1967)
Case study of public television coverage of a social issue (e.g., racism) or health issue (e.g., AIDS)
Challenges facing public television today and in the future
Children's programs on public television
Comparative analysis of different types of licensees of public television stations (i.e., community nonprofit corporations, state commissions, universities, and public school systems)
Comparative analysis of news and documentary programs on public television and commercial television.
Comparative analysis of public television system in the United States with public television system in another country (e.g., the BBC in Great Britain or the NHK in Japan).
Cultural programs on public television
Does public television, as some claim, have a liberal bias?
Economics of fundraising for public television
The evolution of corporate underwriting on public television
Funding for public television
Government criticism on public television
History of *Mister Rogers' Neighborhood*, *Sesame Street* and other pre-school programming on public television
History of your local public television station
How programming decisions are made on public television
Imported programs on public television
Is public television living up to its original mission?

Management and organization of public television stations
Member involvement in public television stations
PBS Adult Learning Service
Political (presidential and congressional) influence on public television
Public television and applications of new technology (e.g., interactive tele-
communications)
Public television in the 21st century
Public television's role in science and math education
Public television's special programming services for the hearing and seeing-
impaired
The relationship between cable television and public broadcasting
The relationship between the Public Broadcasting Service (PBS) and the
Corporation for Public Broadcasting (CPB)
Representation and depiction of ethnic minorities on public television
Should the principles behind the Fairness Doctrine continue to apply to
public television?
Significance of public television in today's media environment
Technological history of the production and distribution of public television
in the United States

Sources

Aufderheide, Patricia. "Public Television and the Public Sphere." *Critical Studies in Mass Communication* (June 1991): 168–83.
Carnegie Commission on the Future of Public Broadcasting. *A Public Trust*. New York: Bantam, 1979.
CPB Public Broadcasting Directory. Washington, DC: Corporation for Public Broadcasting, annual.
Carey, John. *Telecommunications Technologies and Public Broadcasting 1986*. Washington, DC: Corporation for Public Broadcasting, 1986.
Duggan, Ervin. "Where Does the Public Interest Lie?," in *Television for the 21st Century: The Next Wave*. Edited by Charles M. Firestone. Washington, D.C.: The Aspen Institute, 1993.
Frank, Ronald E. and Marshall G. Greenberg. *Audiences for Public Television*. Beverly Hills, CA: Sage, 1982.
Fuller, Linda. *Community Television in the United States: A Sourcebook on Public, Educational, and Governmental Access*. Westport, CT: Greenwood Press, 1994.
Hoynes, William. *Public Television for Sale: Media, the Market, and the Public Sphere*. Boulder, CO: Westview Press, 1994.
Lashley, Marilyn. *Public Television: Panancea, Pork Barrel, or Public Trust?* Westport, CT: Greenwood Press, 1992.
Macy, John W., Jr. *To Irrigate a Wasteland: The Struggle to Shape a Public Television System in the United States*. Berkeley: University of California, 1974.

Pepper, Robert. *The Formation of the Public Broadcasting Service.* New York: Arno Press, 1979.

Robertson, Jim. *TeleVisionaries: In Their Own Words Public Television's Founders Tell How It All Began.* Charlotte Harbor, FL: Tabby House Books, 1993.

Schiller, Herbert I. *Culture, Inc.: The Corporate Takeover of Public Expression.* New York: Oxford University Press, 1989.

Stone, D. *Nixon and the Politics of Public Television.* New York: Garland, 1985.

Twentieth Century Fund Task Force on Public Television. *Quality Time?* New York: Twentieth Century Fund Press, 1993.

Witherspoon, John and Roselle Kovitz. *The History of Public Broadcasting.* Washington, DC: Current, 1987.

REGULATION
AND POLICY

From its inception, broadcast television, perceived primarily as a commercial medium, has been regulated by the Federal Communications Commission (FCC), which was created by the Communications Act of 1934 originally to regulate radio broadcasting. Broadcast television policy and regulation have been largely based on the concept of channel scarcity — that is, there is a limited number of broadcast frequencies in the electromagnetic spectrum. The FCC grants licenses and assigns frequencies to station owners to use the public airwaves to broadcast for the "public convenience, interest, and necessity."

The FCC, as an administrative agency, engages in three basic types of regulation. *Technical regulation* involves such issues as frequency allocation and standardization of new technologies. *Structural regulation* includes rules on issues such as station ownership and program syndication. Finally, *behavioral regulation* refers to the practices affecting television content, ranging from an indecency rule to equal opportunity requirements for political candidates.

In addition to the FCC, all branches of the federal government are involved in television policy, law, and/or regulation. The President nominates FCC commissioners and works with agencies such as the National Telecommunications and Information Administration (NTIA) in the Department of Commerce to develop relevant communication policies. Congress not only confirms FCC commissioners and appropriates funding for the FCC, but it also passes laws to amend and supplement the Communications Act of 1934. Examples of legislative action include the law to ban cigarette advertising on television and the Public Broadcasting Act of 1967 that created public television. The courts also play a significant role, making important decisions about the constitutionality of television-related issues and specific FCC rules.

During the 1980s, the FCC deregulated television broadcasting as cable became more pervasive and the scarcity argument became less valid. The Fairness Doctrine, requiring broadcasters to present both sides of a controversial issue, was repealed. The new policy emphasized free marketplace competition. Thus far in the 1990s, there has been a mixed bag of deregulation (e.g., network production ownership and syndication rules) and re-regulation (e.g., children's television programming and cable television pricing policies). As television converges with telephone and computer technologies, the government will continue to be involved in not only regulating conventional television but also new television-related technologies and services as part of a national telecommunications information infrastructure.

(See also Industry, Technology)

Topic Suggestions

Allocation policy and procedures of electromagnetic spectrum space
Broadcast station licensing rules and public file requirements
Case study of the FCC "freeze" on new television station licensees between 1948 and 1952
Case study of how cigarette advertising was banned from television (*Banzhaf v. FCC*)
Children's television (policy, law and regulation)
Comparative analysis of television regulation in the United States with that in one or more other countries
Deregulation during the Reagan administration
Fairness Doctrine and the First Amendment
Family Hour (a case study exploring the relationship among Congress, the FCC, and the courts)
FCC policy on direct broadcast satellites (DBS)
FCC policy on public service broadcasting
FCC policy on televised sporting events
FCC policy toward minority ownership (Minority Preference Policy)
First Amendment rights of broadcasters vs. the needs and interests of the public (e.g., televised executions)
Government policy on sex and violence on television
Historical analysis of the politics of regulation (relationship among the President, Congress, and the FCC)
Historical influence of public interest groups (e.g., Action for Children's Television) on government policy and regulation
History of cable regulation
History of technical regulation
International regulation of satellites by the International Telecommunication Union (ITU)

Legal aspects of financing and syndicating television productions
National Telecommunications and Information Administration (NTIA)
The 1934 Communications Act: will it survive into the 21st century?
Non-parallel regulations for the broadcasting, cable, and telephone industries
Organizational analysis of Federal Communications Commission (FCC)
Problems in regulating new television technologies (e.g., creating universal standards for HDTV)
Public Broadcasting Service (PBS) policy
Public policy implications of advanced television systems (e.g., convergence of cable television, computer, and telephone technologies)
Regulation of political broadcasts
Regulation of television advertising by the FCC, Federal Trade Commission (FTC), and Food and Drug Administration (FDA)
Regulation vs. deregulation
Regulatory battles between the broadcasting and cable industries (e.g., syndicated exclusivity and must-carry rules)
Self-regulation by the broadcasting and cable industries
Station ownership regulations
Television cameras in the courtroom
Television content regulation (obscenity law and indecency rules)
Television network regulation
U.S. government policy toward international video piracy and other copyright violations

Sources

Association for Education in Journalism and Mass Communication. *First Amendment Issues and the Mass Media: A Bibliography of Recent Works*. Columbia, SC: The Association, 1991.

Barber, Susanna. *News Cameras in the Courtroom: A Free Press—Fair Trial Debate*. Norwood, NJ: Ablex, 1987.

Baughman, James L. *Television's Guardians: The FCC and the Politics of Programming, 1958-1967*. Knoxville, TN: The University of Tennessee Press, 1985.

Bensman, Marvin R. *Broadcast/Cable Regulation*. Lanham, MD. University Press of America, 1990.

Besen, Stanley M. and others. *Misregulating Television: Network Dominance and the FCC*. Chicago: University of Chicago Press, 1984.

Brennan, Timothy J. "The Fairness Doctrine as Public Policy." *Journal of Broadcasting and Electronic Media* (Fall 1989): 419-40.

Brenner, David L. and Monroe E. Price. *Cable Television and Other Non-broadcast Video: Law and Policy*. New York: Clark Boardman, 1986 (updated regularly).

Brightbill, George D. *Communications and the United States Congress: A*

Selectively Annotated Bibliography of Committee Hearings 1870–1976. Washington, DC: Broadcast Education Association, 1978.

Carter, T. Barton, Marc A. Franklin and Jay B. Wright. *The First Amendment and the Fifth Estate: Regulation of Electronic Mass Media.* 2nd ed. Mineola, NY: Foundation Press, 1989.

Chesterman, John and Andy Lipman. *The Electronic Pirates: Crime of the Century.* London: Routledge, 1988.

Code of Federal Regulations. *Title 47: Telecommunications.* 5 vols. Washington, DC: U.S. Government Printing Office. Annual.

Cole, Barry G. and Mal Oettinger. *Reluctant Regulators: The FCC and the Broadcast Audience.* Menlo Park, CA: Addison-Wesley, 1978.

Diamond, Edwin, Norman Sandler and Milton Mueller. *Telecommunications in Crisis: The First Amendment, Technology and Deregulation.* Washington, DC: Cato Institute, 1983.

Donnerstein, Edward, Barbara Wilson and Daniel Linz. "On the Regulation of Broadcast Indecency to Protect Children." *Journal of Broadcasting and Electronic Media* 36 (Winter 1992): 111–117.

Francois, William E. *Mass Media Law and Regulation.* Prospect Heights, IL: Waveland Press, 1994.

Friendly, Fred W. *The Good Guys, the Bad Guys, and the First Amendment: Free Speech vs. Fairness in Broadcasting.* New York: Random House, 1976.

Ginsburg, Douglas H., Michael H. Botein and Mark D. Director. *Regulation of the Electronic Mass Media.* 2nd ed. St. Paul, MN: West Publishing, 1991.

Hilliard, Robert L. *The Federal Communications Commission: A Primer.* Boston: Focal Press, 1991.

Horwitz, Robert Britt. *The Irony of Regulatory Reform: The Deregulation of American Telecommunications.* New York: Oxford University Press, 1989.

Kahn, Frank J., ed. *Documents of American Broadcasting.* 4th ed. Englewood Cliffs, NJ: Prentice-Hall, 1984.

Krasnow, Erwin G. and others. *The Politics of Broadcast Regulation.* 3rd ed. New York: St. Martin's Press, 1982.

Labunski, Richard E. *The First Amendment Under Siege.* Westport, CT: Greenwood Press, 1981.

Le Duc, Don R. *Beyond Broadcasting: Patterns in Policy and Law.* New York: Longman, 1987.

Pember, Don. *Mass Media Law.* 4th ed. Dubuque, IA: Wm. C. Brown, 1987.

Powe, Lucas A. Jr. *American Broadcasting and the First Amendment.* Berkeley: University of California Press, 1987.

Ray, William B. *FCC: The Ups and Downs of Radio-TV Regulation.* Ames: Iowa State University Press, 1990.

Reuben-Cooke, Wilhelmina M. "Rethinking Legal and Policy Paradigms," in *Television for the 21st Century: The Next Wave.* Edited by Charles M. Firestone. Washington, D.C.: The Aspen Institute, 1993.

Rowan, Ford. *Broadcast Fairness: Doctrine, Practice, Prospects: A Reappraisal of the Fairness Doctrine and Equal Time Rule*. New York: Longman, 1984.

Tunstall, Jeremy. *Communications Deregulation: The Unleashing of America's Communications Industry*. New York: Basil Blackwell, 1986.

U.S. Federal Communications Commission. *Annual Report*. Washington, DC: U.S. Government Printing Office. Annual.

RELIGION

Televised religion, sometimes referred to as the "electronic church," appeals to people with spiritual values. Research suggests that religious programming often supplements rather than replaces church-going. Audiences for religious programs tend to be older adults and disproportionately female. This may be because people become more involved in religion as they grow older, the elderly have less mobility to leave the home, and women live statistically, on the average, longer than men. Also worth noting is that while religious television is available in every part of the United States, the largest audiences by far are in the Midwest and South, especially in areas that constitute the traditional "Bible Belt."

Most religious television depends for survival on an audience response that results in contributions from viewers. Television preachers, known as televangelists, buy television time in individual markets and then spend a considerable portion of their program time soliciting financial support. Sophisticated marketing and promotion, including computerized information processing of contributors, have increased electronic church efficiency and profitability.

Critics of religious television condemn the electronic church for its secular aping of non–Christian programming formats. Others question the moral character and motives of televangelists, especially since the highly publicized scandals involving Jim Bakker and Jimmy Swaggart. Finally, some criticize the para-personal relationship viewers have with television preachers as incapable of adequately serving human needs in times of personal crisis.

It is important to recognize that religion on television extends beyond the televangelists. Religion on television includes a broadcast of a local Sunday church service, a satellite telecast of Christmas Mass from the Vatican, a citizen with a religious message on a local cable public access channel, and 24-hour cable and satellite networks. Religious issues are also sometimes covered on secular news and information programs as well as in fictional programming.

Topic Suggestions

Biographical study of one or more televangelists
Case study of a religious television station
Case study of the Reverend Jerry Falwell and his Moral Majority
Comparative analysis of conventional religion and the "electronic church"
Comparative analysis of televised religion in the United States with that in
    one or more other countries
Economic analysis of televised religion
Effects of negative press coverage on audiences of religious programming
Evangelical Council for Financial Accountability
Forms of persuasion used by televangelists
History of religious programming on television
Influence of televised religion on politics
Mail order sales and promotional giveaways on televised religious program-
    ming
Marketing of television religion
Minority (non–Christian) religious programming
Organizational analysis of the National Religious Broadcasters (NRB)
Para-personal communication via religious television (prayer requests,
    counseling hotlines, etc.)
Pat Robertson and the Family Channel
Religious cable and satellite networks
Religious video industry
Representation and depiction of religious characters and issues in television
    dramas and comedies
Rhetorical styles of televangelists
Scandals (the rise and fall of Jim Bakker and Jimmy Swaggart)
Televangelist fraud
Television news coverage of sensitive religious issues such as priests molest-
    ing children
Who watches and why: an audience analysis of religious programming

Sources

Abelman, Robert and Stewart M. Hoover, eds. *Religious Television: Con-
    troversies and Conclusions*. Norwood, NJ: Ablex, 1990.
Bruce, Steve. *Pray TV: Televangelism in America*. London: Routledge, 1990.
Erickson, Hal. *Religious Radio and Television in the United States, 1921–
    1991: The Programs and Personalities*. Jefferson, NC: McFarland,
    1992.
Ferre, John P., ed. *Channels of Belief: Religion and American Commercial
    Television*. Ames: Iowa State University Press, 1990.
Fishwick, Marshall W. and Ray B. Browne, eds. *The God Pumpers:
    Religion in the Electronic Age*. Bowling Green: Bowling Green Univer-
    sity Press, 1987.

Fore, William F. *TV and Religion: The Shaping of Faith, Values and Culture*. Minneapolis: Augsburg, 1987.

Frankl, Razelle. *Televangelism: The Marketing of Popular Religion*. Carbondale: Southern Illinois University Press, 1987.

Goethals, Gregor T. *The Electronic Golden Calf: Images, Religion, and the Making of Meaning*. Cambridge: Cowley Publications, 1990.

Gunter, Barrie and Viney, Rachel. *Seeing Is Believing: Religion and Television in 1990's*. London: John Libbey, 1994.

Hadden, Jeffrey K. and Anson Shupe. *Televangelism: Power and Politics on God's Frontier*. New York: Henry Holt and Company, 1988.

Hadden, Jeffrey K. and Charles E. Swan. *Prime Time Preachers: The Rising Power of Televangelism*. Menlo Park, CA: Addison-Wesley, 1981.

Hill, George H. *Airwaves to the Soul: The Influence and Growth of Religious Broadcasting in America*. Saratoga, CA: R & E Publishers, 1983.

Hill, George H. and Lenwood Davis. *Religious Broadcasting 1920-1983: A Selectively Annotated Bibliography*. New York: Garland, 1984.

Horsfield, Peter G. *Religious Television: The American Experience*. New York: Longman, 1984.

Hoover, Stuart. *Mass Media Religion: The Social Sources of the Electronic Church*. London: Sage, 1988.

James, Hunter. *Smile Pretty and Say Jesus: The Last Great Days of PTL*. Athens: University of Georgia Press, 1993.

Peck, Janice. *The Gods of Televangelism: The Crisis of Meaning and the Appeal of Religious Television*. Cresskill, NJ: Hampton Press, 1993.

Razelle, Frank. *Televangelism: The Marketing of Popular Religion*. Carbondale, IL: Southern Illinois University Press, 1987.

Schultze, Quentin J. *Televangelism and American Culture: The Business of Popular Religion*. Grand Rapids, MI: Baker Book House, 1991.

Shepard, Charles E. *Forgiven: The Rise and Fall of Jim Bakker and the PTL Ministry*. New York: Atlantic Monthly Press, 1992.

Soukup, Paul A., compiler. *Christian Communication: A Bibliographical Survey*. Westport, CT: Greenwood Press, 1989.

SOCIAL ASPECTS

Television is an influential medium in our society. The images and messages of television contribute to our everyday sense of social reality. That is, much of what we see on television represents human social relations. As such, some scholars refer to television as a "significant other" (in addition to parents) in the primary socialization process.

One line of socially related television research looks at the treatment of social issues and social groups in television content, be it advertising, news, or entertainment. For example, there are content analysis studies of how television covers certain issues, such as labor/management disputes. As another example, researchers sometimes analyze a minority group's presence on television in terms of both actual numbers and the ways in which its members are depicted. Other socially related research, popularly called the uses-and-gratifications approach, explores how certain groups in society, such as the elderly, use television in their daily lives.

Another area of research focuses on the role of television as one of many institutions that comprise society. For example, researchers study the relationship of television to other societal institutions, such as education and politics. Some of these studies are structural functionalist in nature, meaning that they examine how television works to maintain and re-create the existing social order. Other studies are of a more critical nature, looking at how television, through form and/or content, tends to perpetuate dominant ideologies and existing inequalities among different socioeconomic classes.

Obviously, there are many social aspects of television, too many to enumerate here. Suffice it to say that the popular mass medium is perceived by some as a potentially powerful agent for social change, while others see it principally as an agent for social control and perpetuating the status quo.

(See also Criticism & Theory, Psychological Aspects)

Topic Suggestions

Changing portrayals of couples in television programming

Comparative analysis of television treatment of a social issues (e.g., AIDS) in the United States and in one or more other countries

Depiction of pro-social and anti-social behavior in prime time television drama

Depiction of the relationship between management and workers at the workplace in television news and entertainment programming

"Did you watch the football game last night?": exploring the social utility function of television

Discussion of social issues in television soap operas

History of the representation of families in television programming

How television influences family communication

Influence of family communication on children's television exposure and understanding

Intergenerational communication in television programming

Juvenile crime on television: what messages are being sent?

Literature review of research on television and aggressive social behavior among teenagers

Portrayals of sitcom families across four decades

Positive influences of television on language development

Representation and depiction of single-parent families on television

Role of television as a significant other in the socialization process

Social stereotyping in television entertainment

Social structural analysis of the relationship between television and another institution (e.g., education, politics, military) as social institutions in the United States

Television: an instrument for social change or social control?

Television and alcohol: advertising, program content, and public concerns

Television as a substitute for social interaction

Television portrayals of social classes

Television, sex, and social learning

Television viewing practices among family members

Sources

Adler, Richard P., ed. *Understanding Television: Essays on Television as a Social and Cultural Force.* New York: Praeger, 1981.

Alali, A. Odasuo, ed. *Mass Media Sex and Adolescent Values: An Annotated Bibliography and Directory of Organizations.* Jefferson, NC: McFarland, 1991.

Brown, Les and Savannah Waring Walker, eds. *Fast Forward: The New Television and American Society: Essays from Channels of Communication.* Kansas City: Andrews and McMeel, 1983.

Bryant, Jennings, ed. *Television and the American Family*. Hillsdale, NJ: Lawrence Erlbaum Associates, 1990.

Cheney, Glenn Alan. *Television in American Society*. New York: Franklin Watts, 1983.

Comstock, George. *Television in America*. 2nd ed. Newbury Park, CA: Sage, 1991.

Comstock, George, et al. *Television and Social Behavior: A Technical Report to the Surgeon General's Scientific Advisory Committee on Television and Social Behavior*. Washington, DC: Government Printing Office, 1972.

Gerbner, George. "Science or Ritual Dance? A Revisionist View of Television Violence Effects Research." *Journal of Communication* (Summer 1984): 164–73.

Goldberg, Kim. *The Barefoot Channel: Community TV as a Tool for Social Change*. Vancouver: New Star Books, 1990.

Goodwin, Andrew and Garry Whannel, editors. *Understanding Television*. London: Routledge, 1990.

Lull, James. *Inside Family Viewing: Ethnographic Research on Television's Audiences*. London: Routledge, 1990.

Meyrowitz, Joshua. *No Sense of Place: The Impact of Electronic Media on Social Behavior*. New York: Oxford University Press, 1985.

Montgomery, Kathryn C. *Target Prime Time: Advocacy Groups and the Struggle Over Entertainment Television*. New York: Oxford University Press, 1989.

Morley, David. *Family TV: Cultural Power and Domestic Leisure*. London: Comedia, 1986.

Oskamp, S. *Television as a Social Issue*. Newbury Park, CA: Sage, 1988.

Rowland, Willard, Jr. *The Politics of TV Violence*. Beverly Hills, CA: Sage, 1983.

Schwartz, Meg, ed. *TV & Teens: Experts Look at the Issues*. Reading, MA: Addison-Wesley, 1982.

Silverstone, Roger. *Television and Everyday Life*. New York: Routledge, 1994.

Spigel, Lynn. *Making Room for TV: Television and the Family Ideal in Postwar America*. Chicago: University of Chicago Press, 1992.

Taylor, Ella. *Prime-Time Families: TV Culture in Postwar America*. Berkeley: University of California Press, 1989.

Thaler, Paul. *The Watchful Eye: American Justice in the Age of the Television Trial*. Westport: CT: Praeger, 1994.

Zillmann, Dolf, Jennings Bryant and Aletha Huston, eds. *Media, Children, and the Family*. Hillsdale, NJ: Lawrence Erlbaum Associates, 1993.

SPORTS

Televised sporting events have evolved significantly since the first event, a 1939 baseball game between Princeton and Columbia. Few would have predicted that this first event, using rather crude methods and featuring only one camera, would lead to the current relationship between television and sports, one that includes all-sports channels. Today, countless more Americans watch televised sports than attend live events. The television and sports industries are involved in a multibillion dollar-a-year symbiotic relationship, one in which television has influenced the very games it covers.

Effects of television upon sports are far ranging. Professional sports can be virtually live or die by whether or not they receive television coverage. Television executives, working in conjunction with league officials, often conspire to change both the starting times and scheduling of sporting events. Games played at night are more likely to gather higher ratings, and as a result, more games are being moved to prime time. For example, baseball has become increasingly dominated by night games, illustrated by the fact that the World Series is now played entirely at night. The rules of games have also been altered, as in the case of baseball's designated hitter, to provide television viewers with a theoretically more exciting offensive game.

A large percentage of sports programming continues to revolve around the big three of baseball, football, and basketball. These sports provide the right forum for television in regards to the tempo and nature of the game, breaks for advertising, and marquee players for promotion. Other sports lack these qualities, and as a result have not received equal television exposure. Soccer, the worlds most popular sport, receives little exposure on U.S. television because teams score few goals, and no stoppages during play translates into few opportunities for commercials. However, the future of televised sports will most likely include a greater volume and variety of sports coverage, as well as a move toward more pay-per-view programming.

Controversies arising out of the relationship between television and sports include problems of viewer access ("free" broadcast television vs. pay cable), gender inequities (less coverage and prize money for female sports) and revenue sharing (teams in small television markets unable to earn as much in television license fees as large market teams, and therefore having fewer resources to compete for free-agent players).

Topic Suggestions

Advanced television-related technology and sports
Cable sports networks (e.g., ESPN)
Case history of the failed United States Football League (USFL) and its dependency on television
Challenges of producing and directing a live televised sporting event
Comparative analysis of televised sports in the United States and in one or more other countries
Comparative analysis of the experience of viewing televised sports and live attendance at sporting events
Cultural analysis of the Super Bowl
Economic aspects of television sports
Effects of television sports on youth
Gender inequity in television sports coverage
Historical overview of how television has influenced sports
History of television coverage of a particular sport (e.g., golf)
History of television sports announcing
Impact of pay-per-view television on professional sports
Relationship between television networks and the College Football Association
Sports programming created specifically for television (e.g., wrestling)
Role of television in professional sports labor disputes
Television coverage of the Olympic Games
Uses and gratifications of television sports fans

Sources

Barnett, Steven. *Games and Sets: The Changing Face of Sport on Television*. London: BFI, 1990.
Chad, Norman. *Hold on Honey, I'll Take You to the Hospital at Halftime: Confessions of a TV Sports Junkie*. New York: Atlantic Monthly Press, 1993.
Chandler, Joan M. *TV and National Sport: The United States and Great Britain*. Urbana: University of Illinois Press, 1989.
Gunther, Marc and Bill Carter. *Monday Night Mayhem: The Inside Story of ABC's Monday Night Football*. New York: William Morrow, 1988.

Hitchcock, John R. *Sportscasting*. Boston: Focal Press, 1991.

Klatell, David A. and Norman Marcus. *Sports for Sale: Television, Money, and the Fans*. New York: Oxford University Press, 1988.

O'Neil, Terry. *The Game Behind the Game: High Stakes, High Pressures in TV Sports*. New York: Harper and Row, 1989.

Patton, Phil. *Razzle Dazzle: The Curious Marriage of Television and Professional Football*. Garden City, NY: Doubleday, 1984.

Powers, Ron. *Supertube: The Rise of Television Sports*. New York: Coward-McCann, 1984.

Rader, Benjamin G. *In Its Own Image: How Television Has Transformed Sports*. New York: Free Press, 1984.

Real, Michael R. "The Super Bowl: Mythical Spectacle." *Journal of Communication* 25 (Winter 1975): 31–43.

Smith, Curt. *Voices of the Game: The First Full-Scale Overview of Baseball Broadcasting, 1921 to the Present*. South Bend, IN: Diamond Communication, 1987.

Staudohar, Paul D. *The Sports Industry and Collective Bargaining*. Ithaca, NY: ILR Press, 1986.

Wenner, Lawrence A., ed. *Media, Sports, and Society*. Newbury Park, CA: Sage, 1989.

Whannel, Garry. *Fields in Vision: TV Sport and Cultural Transformation*. London: Routledge, 1992.

Wyche, Mark C., James M. Trautman and Paul I. Bortz. *Sports on Television: A New Ball Game for Broadcasters*. Washington: National Association of Broadcasters, 1990.

TECHNOLOGY

The word "television" first appeared in 1907 in an issue of the *Scientific American*. However, inventors and scientists were at work even in the previous century, exploring the possibility of sending pictures over a distance. For example, in 1884, German Paul Nipkow patented his Nipkow disk, an "electrical telescope" that is credited as an early major technological discovery that images could travel, in this case via wires, over distances. Two Americans, working in the 20th century, are recognized as the major contributors toward making television broadcasting a reality by 1939. Vladimir Zworykin created an all-electronic system to transform visual images into electronic signals, and Philo Farnsworth developed a cathode ray tube that used an electronic scanner to reproduce electronic images.

For most of its history, television has employed broadcasting technology to distribute signals from station transmitters to home antennas and receivers. Broadcasting uses the air waves, which are electromagnetic radiations traveling at the speed of light, as the channel for communications. Cable technology, which uses wires to deliver television to homes, was first used in the 1940s but did not become popular until decades later when satellite technology made it possible for cable system operators to acquire programming inexpensively and with greater efficiency. Direct broadcast satellite (DBS) technology in the 1970s and 1980s made it possible for people unable to receive traditional broadcast signals and not hooked to cable to receive television by installing earth-receiving satellite dishes on or near their homes.

VCR technology added still another way for people to watch television. Beyond distribution, technological developments in the history of television have encompassed all areas, ranging from production (e.g., cameras) to recording (e.g., tape) to exhibition (e.g., monitors). Today, we are witnessing the convergence of several technologies — particularly television, computer, and telephone — that will lead to an advanced television of the future that is both fully interactive and digital.

The Federal Communications Commission is primarily responsible for regulating television technology in the United States. For example, the FCC has made important policy decisions on technological issues such as broadcast and color television standards, the uses of the VHF and UHF bands of the electro-magnetic spectrum, low-power television stations (LPTV), stereo television, and high-definition television (HDTV). Unfortunately, there is no universal broadcast television standard at the global level, where three incompatible television systems exist (the U.S.-originated NTSC, the German-originated PAL, and the French-originated SECAM).

Topic Suggestions

Analog broadcasting vs. digital video
Case history of the regulatory battle over an industry standard for color television
Case history of the Warner-Amex Qube system
Case study of technology involved in broadcasting the Super Bowl
The chief engineer's responsibilities at a television station
Comparative analysis of world broadcasting standards (NTSC, PAL, and SECAM)
Convergence of television, computer, and telephone technologies
Direct Broadcast Satellite (DBS)
Economic analysis of building the technological infrastructure needed to connect television to the "information highway"
Educational applications of state-of-the-art television-related technology (multimedia)
Ethical considerations of new communications technologies
Evolution of use of computers in television station operations
Fiber optics
High-definition television (HDTV)
History of broadcasting technology
History of cable technology
History of government policy toward and FCC regulation of new television-related technologies
History of television animation technology
History of television camera technology
History of television set technology
History of videotape technology
How interactive television works
How the camcorder changed the nature of television
Impact of technology on television news reporting
Impact of telecommunications technologies on global politics
Information service technologies: (videotex, teletext, etc.)

International technical regulation of the electromagnetic spectrum (World
    Administrative Radio Conferences)
Low-power television (LPTV)
Medical applications of state-of-the-art television-related technology
Satellite Master Antenna Systems (SMATV)
Scientific and engineering breakthroughs in the development of television
Stereo television
Technological analysis of television special effects
Technological history of networks
Teleconferencing
Television and three-dimensional holography
Television image scramblers and decoders
Television news coverage of science and technology
Television, video games, and virtual reality
Wireless cable

Sources

Acampora, Anthony S. *An Introduction to Broadband Networks: LANs,
    MANs, ATM, B-ISDN, and Optical Networks for Integrated
    Multimedia Telecommunications.* New York: Plenum, 1994.
Alber, Antone. *Interactive Computer Systems: Videotex and Multimedia.*
    New York: Plenum, 1993.
Arlen, Gary H., et al. *Tomorrow's TVs: A Review of New TV Set Tech-
    nology, Related Video Equipment, and Potential Market Impacts,
    1987–1995.* Washington, D.C.: National Association of Broadcasters,
    1987.
Aumente, Jerome. *New Electronic Pathways: Videotex, Teletext, and
    Online Databases.* Newbury Park: Sage, 1987.
Benson, K. Blair. *Television Engineering Handbook.* New York: McGraw-
    Hill, 1986.
Binkowski, Edward. *Satellite Information Systems.* Boston: G.K. Hall,
    1988.
Chaffee, C. David. *The Rewiring of America: The Fiber Optics Revolution.*
    Orlando, FL: Academic Press, 1988.
Chetty, P.R. *Satellite Technology & Its Applications.* 2nd ed. Blue Ridge
    Summit, PA: TAB Books, 1991.
Dizard, Wilson P., Jr. *The Coming Information Age: An Overview of Tech-
    nology, Economics and Politics.* 3rd ed. New York: Longman, 1989.
Dordick, Herbert S. *Understanding Modern Telecommunications.* New
    York: McGraw-Hill, 1986.
Ellis, David. *Split Screen: Home Entertainment and the New Technologies.*
    Toronto: Friends of Canadian Broadcasting, 1992.
Gilder, George F. *Life After Television: The Coming Transformation of
    Media and American Life.* Rev. ed. New York: W. W. Norton, 1994.

Gross, Lynne Schafer. *The New Television Technologies*. 3rd ed. Dubuque, IA: Wm. C. Brown, 1990.

Hanson, Jarice. *Connections: Technologies in Communications*. New York: Harper Collins College Publishers, 1994.

Hilsman, Hoyt R. *The New Electronic Media: Innovations in Video Technologies*. Boston: Focal Press, 1989.

Hudson, Heather E. *Communication Satellites: Their Development and Impact*. New York: Free Press, 1990.

Inglis, Andrew F. *Behind the Tube: A History of Broadcasting Technology and Business*. Boston: Focal Press, 1990.

Inglis, Andrew F. *Satellite Technology: An Introduction*. Boston: Focal Press, 1991.

Jones, Maxine Holmes. *See, Hear, Interact: Beginning Developments in Two-way Television*. Metuchen, NJ: Scarecrow Press, 1985.

Kraeuter, David W. *Radio and Television Pioneers: A Patent Bibliography*. Metchuen, NJ: Scarecrow Press, 1992.

Long, Mark, compiler. *World Satellite Almanac*. 3rd ed. Winter Beach, FL: MLE Inc., 1992.

Luther, Sara Lethcher. *The United States and the Direct Broadcast Satellite: The Politics of International Broadcasting in Space*. New York: Oxford University Press, 1988.

Mirabito, Michael M. and Barbara L. Morgenstern. *The New Communications Technologies*. 2nd ed. Boston: Focal Press, 1994.

Mosco, Vincent. *The Pay-Per Society: Computers and Communication in the Information Age*. Toronto: Garamond Press, 1989.

Mosco, Vincent. *Pushbutton Fantasies: Critical Perspectives on Videotext and Information Technology*. Norwood, NJ: Ablex, 1982.

Neuman, W. Russell. "The Technological Convergence: Television Networks and Telephone Networks," in *Television for the 21st Century: The Next Wave*. Edited by Charles M. Firestone. Washington, D.C.: The Aspen Institute, 1993.

Noll, A. Michael. *Television Technology: Fundamentals and Future Prospects*. Norwood, MA: Artech, 1988.

Pool, Ithiel de Sola and Eli M. Noam, eds. *Technologies Without Boundaries: On Telecommunications in a Global Age*. Cambridge, MA: Harvard University Press, 1990.

Prentiss, Stan. *HDTV: High-Definition Television*. 2nd ed. Blue Ridge Summit, PA: TAB Books, 1994.

Reed, David P. *Residential Fiber Optic Networks: An Engineering and Economic Analysis*. Norwood, MA: Artech House, 1992.

Rees, David W. *Satellite Communications: The First Quarter Century of Service*. New York: John Wiley & Sons, 1990.

Rice, John F., ed. *HDTV: The Politics, Policies, and Economics of Tomorrow's Television*. New York: Union Square Press, 1990.

Roddy, Dennis. *Satellite Communications*. New York: Prentice Hall, 1989.

Rzeszewski, Theodore S., ed. *Television Technology Today*. New York: Institute of Electrical and Electronics Engineers, 1985.

Shiers, George, ed. *Technical Development of Television*. New York: Arno, 1977.

Singleton, Loy A. *Global Impact: The New Telecommunications Technologies*. New York: Harper and Row, 1989.

Singleton, Loy A. *Telecommunications in the Information Age: A Nontechnical Primer on the New Technologies*. 2nd ed. Cambridge, MA: Ballinger, 1986.

Sudalnik, James and Victoria Kuhl, compilers. *High-Definition Television: An Annotated Multidisciplinary Bibliography, 1981–1992*. Westport, CT: Greenwood Press, 1994.

Sutpin, S.E. *Understanding Satellite Television Reception*. Englewood Cliffs, NJ: Prentice-Hall, 1986.

Tirro, Sebastiano. ed. *Satellite Communication Systems Design*. New York: Plenum, 1993.

White, Rita Lauria and Harold M. White, Jr. *The Law and Regulation of International Space Communication*. Norwood, MA: Artech House, 1988.

Wilson, Kevin G. *Technologies of Control*. Madison: University of Wisconsin Press, 1989.

World Satellite Directory. Potomac, MD: Phillips Publishing. Annual.

VIDEO

In 1956, CBS was the first network to use a video tape recorder, which was manufactured by Ampex Corporation. A decade later, Sony introduced the first mobile video system, and in the 1970s Philips marketed the first VCR for home use. The 1970s and 1980s marked years of great competition and growth for the video industry. During this time, VHS emerged as the victorious video format over Sony's Betamax tape and videodisc technology, and television news operations and other production switched from film to videotape.

The video software market today includes popular movies, pornography, children's video ("kidvid"), and exercise videos. By the end of the 1980s, prerecorded video sales and rentals in the United States generated revenue comparable to motion picture box office receipts. In the 1990s the prerecorded video industry continues to prosper but also faces lost revenue from the persistent problem of international piracy as well as the from the challenge of new interactive television services, specifically movies-on-demand (also known as video-dialtone).

Video technology allows individuals to schedule their programming by recording programs and watching them whenever they wish, a process known as "timeshifting." In 1984, the U.S. Supreme Court ruled in a suit brought by MCA and Disney against Sony that such home taping does not violate copyright laws. Video camcorders also allow people to be producers themselves, and several television programs, including *America's Funniest Home Videos,* have featured this phenomenon.

In addition to entertainment, video is used for a myriad of reasons, including school instruction, business training, videoconferencing, psychological feedback therapy, and security purposes. Video technology has become more compact, portable, and affordable over the last two decades. The future will bring higher-definition video as a result of a shift from analog to digital technology. We can also expect new and/or improved video products, such as the video telephone.

Topic Suggestions

Aesthetic comparison of viewing movies on video at home versus viewing movies on film in theaters

Amateur video from news footage to entertainment on television

Analog versus digital video

Analysis of a particular video genre (e.g., sports videos)

Applications of interactive video (multimedia) technology

Children's uses and gratifications of home VCRs

Comparative analysis of videotape and videodisc technologies

Corporate television

Cultural impact of VCR diffusion in developing parts of the world

Developing and maintaining video collections in libraries

Direct marketing of videotapes

Economic analysis of the video rental industry

Economic impact of pay-per-view and video-on-demand television on the video rental industry

Historical analysis of how video technology has changed television news-gathering

Historical analysis of the relationship between the video and the motion picture industries

The erotic and pornographic video industry

Historical overview of the evolution of the video camera

Organizational history of Blockbuster Video

Psychological uses of video feedback

Shooting weddings: videography as an entrepreneurial business

Survey of uses of institutional video

Timeshifting: how video has changed television viewing habits

Use of video in the security industry

VHS versus Betamax: a case history of competing video technologies

Video games: past, present, and future

Video industry pricing strategies for pre-recorded videotapes

Video piracy in the United States and around the world

Video press releases: another form of propaganda?

Video used for surveillance

Videoconferencing

Sources

Alvarado, Manuel, ed. *Video World Wide: An International Study*. London: John Libbey, 1988.

Armes, Roy. *On Video*. London: Routledge, 1988.

Budd, John F. *Corporate Video in Focus: A Management Guide to Private TV*. Englewood Cliffs, NJ: Prentice-Hall, 1983.

Carlberg, Scott. *Corporate Video Survival*. White Plains, NY: Knowledge Industry Publications, 1991.

Cartwright, Steve R. *Secrets of Successful Video Training*. White Plains, NY: Knowledge Industry Publications, 1990.

Cubitt, Sean. *Timeshift: On Video Culture*. London: Routledge, 1991.

Cubitt, Sean. *Videography: Video Media as Art and Culture*. New York: St. Martin's Press, 1993.

DiZazzo, Ray. *Corporate Television: A Producer's Handbook*. Boston: Focal Press, 1990.

DiZazzo, Ray. *Directing Corporate Video*. Boston: Focal Press, 1993.

Dobrow, Julia, ed. *Social and Cultural Aspects of VCR Use*. Hillsdale, NJ: Lawrence Erlbaum Associates, 1990.

Dranov, Paula. *Video in the 80's*. White Plains, NY: Knowledge Industry Publications, 1980.

Eustace, Grant. *Writing for Corporate Videos*. Boston: Focal Press, 1990.

Ganley, Gladys D. *The Exploding Power of Personal Media*. Norwood, NJ: Ablex, 1992.

Ganley, Gladys D. and Oswald H. Ganley. *Global Political Fallout: The VCR's First Decade 1976–85*. Norwood, NJ: Ablex, 1987.

Gray, Ann. *Video Playtime: The Gendering of a Leisure Technology*. New York: Routledge, 1992.

Hall, Howard. *Corporate Video Directing*. Boston: Focal Press, 1993.

Hanhardt, John G. *Video Culture: A Critical Investigation*. New York: Workshop Press, 1986.

Hausman, Carl. *Institutional Video: Planning, Budgeting, Production and Evaluation*. Belmont, CA: Wadsworth, 1991.

Iuppa, Nicholas V. *Corporate Video Producer's Handbook*. White Plains, NY: Knowledge Industry Publications, 1993.

Kallenberger, Richard H. and George D. Cvjetnicanin. *Film into Video: A Guide to Merging the Technologies*. Boston: Focal Press, 1994.

Krugman, Dean M., et al. "Video Movies at Home: Are They Viewed Like Film or Like Television?" *Journalism Quarterly* (Spring/Summer 1991): 120–130.

Lardner, James. *Fast Forward: Hollywood, the Japanese and the VCR Wars*. New York: W.W. Norton, 1987.

Levy, Mark, ed. *The VCR Age: Home Video and Mass Communication*. Newbury Park, CA: Sage, 1989.

Levy, Mark and B. Gunter. *Home Video and the Changing Nature of the TV Audience*. London: John Libbey, 1988.

McBride, Donald L., compiler. *Doctoral Dissertations about Videotape and Videodisc: A Bibliography*. Carbondale: Southern Illinois University. Department of Radio and Television, 1989.

Marlow, Eugene and Eugene Secunda. *Shifting Time and Space: The Story of Videotape*. Westport, CT: Praeger, 1991.

Morgan, Michael, Alison Alexander and James Shanahan. "Adolescents, VCR's, and the Family Environment." *Communication Research* 17 (February 1990): 83–96.

Nmungwun, Aaron Foisi. *Video Recording Technology: Its Impact on*

Media and Home Entertainment. Hillsdale, NJ: Lawrence Erlbaum Associates, 1989.

Richardson, Alan. *Corporate and Organizational Video*. New York: McGraw Hill, 1992.

Scholtz, James C. *Video Policies and Procedures for Libraries*. Santa Barbara, CA: ABC-CLIO, 1991.

Stokes, Judith. *The Business of Nonbroadcast Television: Corporate & Institutional Video Budgets, Facilities & Applications*. White Plains, NY: Knowledge Industry Publications, 1988.

Watkinson, John. *The Art of Digital Video*. 2nd ed. Boston: Focal Press, 1994.

WOMEN

In a less sexist society, this conceptual category would be more appropriately called "gender." Although women constitute the gender majority in the United States, they have not been treated as social equals, and this treatment has been reflected in the television viewing experience, televised images, and in the television industry itself. For example, research suggests that women watch more television than men, but men are featured in greater numbers on television. When men and women watch together, men have greater power and control over program choice. Men and women also tend to have different program preferences, viewing styles, and television-related talk behavior.

The depiction of women on television series has changed dramatically over the years, largely mirroring social changes in gender relationships. In the 1950s, women on prime time television were mostly homemakers and played roles supportive of male characters. As the women's movement gained force, television began to feature more stories of working women in lead roles. In the course of 20 years, television evolved from the perfect mother (e.g., June Cleaver on *Leave It to Beaver*), to the single and independent career woman (e.g., Mary Richards on *Mary Tyler Moore*). Another two decades would bring stories of a professional journalist deciding to have a baby out of wedlock (*Murphy Brown*), and an assertive working class woman getting kissed by another woman in a gay bar (*Roseanne*).

Despite changes in women's social roles, certain negative stereotypes continue to exist. For example, sexist portrayals of women are regularly featured in music videos, beer commercials, and video pornography, continuing the objectification of the female body for male pleasure. The gorgeous-but-dumb woman is another lingering stereotype. Today the Lifetime Television cable network targets women for its programming, offering less sexist fare ranging from reruns of favorite broadcast network programs to original movies and a women's weekly news magazine program.

Women have made considerable progress in gaining employment in the television industry, but statistics suggest that most women are still being paid less for the same work that men do. This apparent discrimination extends beyond pay to the types of opportunities made available to women. While changes appear to be coming slowly, it is not difficult to discern the continuing strength of an "old boy's network" in television production companies and the upper levels of management in many stations and networks.

(See Audience, Minorities)

Topic Suggestions

Biographical study of a significant woman in history of television production (e.g., Susan Harris)
Comparative analysis of gender preferences in television program selection
Comparative analysis of the depiction of women on television in the United States and in one or more other countries
Depiction of female character roles in Saturday morning cartoons
Depiction of mother roles in television dramas
Depiction of working women in television sitcoms
The female phenomenon of fan worship of television stars
Feminist theory and television aesthetics
From Lucy to Roseanne: funny ladies on television
History of gender discrimination in television industry employment practices
History of women in television news
How does television cover women's issues?
How does television define female desire?
Psychological impact of women watching violence against women on television
Sex role stereotyping on television from the 1950s to the 1990s
Targeting a female audience on Lifetime Television: a case study of cable network narrowcasting
Video pornography and the objectification of women
Women in television advertising
Women in television management
Women in television sports
Women on daytime television

Sources

Bacon-Smith, Camille. *Enterprising Women: Television Fandom and the Creation of Popular Myth*. Philadelphia: University of Pennsylvania Press, 1992.

Baehr, Helen and Gillian Dyer, eds. *Boxed In: Women and TV*. New York: Pandora, 1987.

Bartel, Diane. *Putting on Appearances: Gender and Advertising*. Philadelphia: Temple University Press, 1988.

Beasley, Maurine H. and Sheila J. Gibbons. *Taking Their Place: A Documentary History of Women and Journalism*. Washington: American University Press, 1993.

Brown, Mary Ellen. *Soap Opera and Women's Talk*. Thousand Oaks, CA: Sage, 1994.

Brown, Mary Ellen, ed. *Television and Women's Culture: The Politics of the Popular*. Newbury Park, CA: Sage, 1990.

Creedon, Pamela J., ed. *Women, Media, and Sport: Challenging Gender Values*. Thousand Oaks, CA: Sage, 1994.

Creedon, Pamela J., ed. *Women in Mass Communication*. 2nd ed. Thousand Oaks, CA: Sage, 1993.

D'Acci, Julie. *Defining Women: Television and the Case of Cagney & Lacey*. Chapel Hill: University of North Carolina Press, 1994.

Douglas, Susan J. *Where the Girls Are: Growing Up Female with the Mass Media*. New York: Times Books, 1994.

Friedman, Leslie J. *Sex Roles Stereotyping in the Mass Media: An Annotated Bibliography*. New York: Garland, 1977.

Gamman, Lorraine and Margaret Marshment, eds. *The Female Gaze: Women as Viewers of Popular Culture*. Seattle: The Real Comet Press, 1989.

Geraghty, Christine. *Women and Soap Opera: A Study of Prime Time Soaps*. Cambridge: Polity, 1991.

Gerbner, George and Nancy Signorielli. *Women and Minorities in Television Drama, 1969–1978: A Research Report*. Philadelphia: University of Pennsylvania Annenberg School of Communication, 1979.

Gray, Ann. *Video Playtime: The Gendering of a Leisure Technology*. London: Routledge, 1992.

Gunter, Barry. *TV and Sex Role Stereotyping*. London: John Libbey, 1986.

Hill, George, Lorraine Raglin and Chas Floyd Johnson. *Black Women in Television: An Illustrated History and Bibliography*. New York: Garland Publishing, 1990.

Hosley, David H. and Gayle K. Yamada. *Hard News: Women in Broadcast Journalism*. Westport, CT: Greenwood Press, 1987.

Kaplan, E. Ann. *Motherhood and Representation: The Mother in Popular Culture and Melodrama*. London: Routledge, 1992.

Krishnan, Prabha and Anita Dighe. *Affirmation and Denial: Construction of Femininity on Indian Television*. London: Sage, 1990.

Lent, John A., compiler. *Women and Mass Communications: An International Annotated Bibliography*. Westport, CT: Greenwood Press, 1991.

Lewis, Lisa A. "Form and Female Authorship in Music Video," in *Television: The Critical View*. 5th ed. Edited by Horace Newcomb. New York: Oxford University Press, 1994.

Lewis, Lisa A. *Gender Politics and MTV: Voicing the Difference*. Philadelphia: Temple University Press, 1990.

Martin, Linda and Kerry Segrave. *Women in Comedy*. Secaucus, NJ: Citadel Press, 1986.

Meehan, Diana M. *Ladies of the Evening: Women Characters of Prime Time Television*. Metuchen, NJ: Scarecrow Press, 1983.

Mellencamp, Patricia. *High Anxiety: Catastrophe, Scandal, Age, and Comedy*. Bloomington: Indiana University Press, 1992.

Morley, David. "Television and Gender," in *Television: The Critical View*. 5th ed. Edited by Horace Newcomb. New York: Oxford University Press, 1994.

Nochimson, Martha. *No End to Her: Soap Opera and the Female Subject*. Berkeley: University of California Press, 1992.

Paisner, Daniel. *The Imperfect Mirror: Inside Stories of Television Newswomen*. New York: Morrow, 1989.

Press, Andrea L. *Women Watching Television: Gender, Class, and Generation in the American Television Experience*. Philadelphia: University of Pennsylvania Press, 1991.

Pribram, E. Deidre, ed. *Female Spectators: Looking at Film & Television*. New York: Routledge, 1988.

Sanders, Marlene and Marcia Rock. *Waiting for Prime Time: The Women of TV News*. New York: Harper and Row, 1988.

Schlesinger, Philip, et al. *Women Viewing Violence*. Bloomington: Indiana University Press, 1992.

Signorielli, Nancy. *Role Portrayal and Stereotyping on Television: An Annotated Bibliography of Studies Relating to Women, Minorities, Aging, Sexual Behavior, Health and Handicaps*. Westport, CT: Greenwood Press, 1985.

Smith, Ronald L. *Sweethearts of '60s TV*. New York: St. Martin's Press, 1989.

Spigel, L. and D. Mann, eds. *Privates Screenings: Television and the Female Consumer*. Minneapolis: University of Minnesota Press, 1992.

Trotta, Liz. *Fighting for Air: In the Trenches with Television News*. New York: Simon & Schuster, 1991.

Tuchman, Gaye, Arlene Kaplan and James Benet. *Hearth and Home: Images of Women in the Mass Media*. New York: Oxford University Press, 1978.

Van Zoonen, Liesbet. *Feminist Media Studies*. Thousand Oaks, CA: Sage, 1994.

Window Dressing on the Set: Women and Minorities in Television: A Report of the United States Commission on Civil Rights. Washington, DC: U.S. Commission on Civil Rights, 1977.

ADDITIONAL SOURCES

Bibliographies

Block, Eleanor S. and James K. Bracken. *Communication and the Mass Media: A Guide to the Reference Literature.* Englewood, CO: Libraries Unlimited, 1991.

Blum, Eleanor and Frances G. Wilhoit. *Mass Media Bibliography: An Annotated Guide to Books and Journals for Research and Reference.* Urbana, University of Illinois, 1990.

Cassata, Mary and Thomas Skill. *Television: A Guide to the Literature.* Phoenix, AZ: Oryx Press, 1988.

Danielson, Wayne A. and G. C. Wilhoit, Jr., compilers. *A Computerized Bibliography of Mass Communication Research, 1944–1964.* New York: Magazine Publishers Association, 1967.

Hill, Susan M., ed. *Broadcasting Bibliography: A Guide to the Literature of Radio and Television.* 3rd. ed. Washington: National Association of Broadcasters, 1989.

Kittross, John M., compiler. *A Bibliography of Theses and Dissertations in Broadcasting 1920–1973.* Washington, DC: Broadcast Education Association, 1978.

McCavitt, William E., compiler. *Radio and Television: A Selected, Annotated Bibliography.* Metuchen, NJ: Scarecrow Press, 1978. *Supplement One, 1977–1981,* 1982.

New Books in the Communications Library (A quarterly annotated bibliography published by the Communications Library at the University of Illinois).

Pringle, Peter K. and Helen E. Clinton. *Radio & Television: A Selected, Annotated Bibliography; Supplement Two: 1982–1986.* Metuchen, NJ: Scarecrow Press, 1989.

Research Methods and Strategies

Gaunt, Philip, ed. *Beyond Agendas: New Directions in Communication Research.* Westport, CT: Greenwood Publishing, 1993.

Lowery, Shearon and Melvin De Fleur. *Milestones in Mass Communication Research.* 2nd ed. New York: Longman, 1988.

Rowland, W.D. and B. Watkins, eds. *Interpreting Television: Current Research Perspectives: Sage Annual Review of Communication Research — Volume 12*. Newbury Park, CA: Sage, 1984.

Rubin, R. B., Rubin A. M. and Piele, L. J. *Communication Research: Strategies and Sources*. 3rd ed. Belmont, CA: Wadsworth, 1993.

Singletary, Michael. M*ass Communication Research: Contemporary Methods and Applications*. New York: Longman, 1994.

Ward, Jean and Kathleen A. Hansen. *Search Strategies in Mass Communication*. 2nd ed. New York: Longman, 1993.

Wimmer, Roger D. and Joseph R. Dominick. *Mass Media Research: An Introduction*. Belmont, CA: Wadsworth, 1991.

Dictionaries and Encyclopedias

Barnouw, Erik, ed. *International Encyclopedia of Communications*. (4 volumes) New York: Oxford University Press, 1989.

Brown, Les. *Les Brown's Encyclopedia of Television*. 3rd ed. Detroit: Visible Ink Press, 1992.

Diamant, Lincoln, ed. *The Broadcast Communications Dictionary*. 3rd. ed. Westport, CT: Greenwood Press, 1989.

Penney, Edmund F. *The Facts on File Dictionary of Film and Broadcast Terms*. New York: Facts on File, 1991.

Directories and Guides

Contemporary Theatre, Film, and Television: A Biographical Guide Featuring Performers, Directors, Writers, Producers, Designers, Managers, Choreographers, Technicians, Composers, Executives, Dancers, and Critics in the United States and Great Britain. 12 volumes. Detroit: Gale Research, 1994.

Fisher, Kim N. *On the Screen: A Film, Television and Video Research Guide*. Littleton, CO: Libraries Unlimited, 1986.

Godfrey, Donald, compiler. *Reruns on File: A Guide to Electronic Media Archives*. Hillsdale, NJ: Lawrence Erlbaum Associates, 1992.

Rouse, Sarah and Katherine Loughney, compilers for the Library of Congress (Motion Picture, Broadcasting, and Recorded Sound Division). *Three Decades of Television: A Catalog of Television Programs Acquired by the Library of Congress, 1949–1979*. Washington, DC: Library of Congress, 1989.

Sterling, Christopher H. *Electronic Media: A Guide to Trends in Broadcasting and Newer Technologies 1920–1983*. New York: Praeger, 1984.

Ulrich's International Periodicals Directory: A Classified Guide to Current Periodicals, Foreign and Domestic. New York: Bowker, biennial.

Annuals

Broadcasting & Cable Yearbook. Washington DC: Broadcasting Publications, Inc., annual (includes a section on books on broadcasting, cable and mass media).
Communication Yearbook. Thousand Oaks, CA: Sage, annual.
International Television & Video Almanac. New York: Quigley Publishing, annual.
Television & Cable Factbook: The Authoritative Reference for the Television, Cable & Electronics Industries. Washington, D.C.: Warren Publishing, annual.
Who's Who in Television. Beverly Hills, CA: Packard Publishing, annual.
Working Press of the Nation TV and Radio Directory. New Providence, NJ: Reed Publishing, annual.
World Radio TV Handbook. New York: Billboard Press, annual.

Abstracts, Indexes, and Databases

Arts and Humanities Citation Index
Business Index
Business Periodicals Index
CBS News Index
COMINDEX
Communication Abstracts
Current Index to Journals in Education
DIALOG
Dissertation Abstracts International Index
Humanities Index
Index to Legal Periodicals
InfoTrac
Journalism Abstracts
Journalism Monographs
Music Index
The New York Times Index
NEXIS
Popular Periodicals Index
Psychological Abstracts
Public Affairs Information Service Bulletin
Reader's Guide to Periodical Literature
Resources in Education (ERIC)
Social Sciences Citation Index
Social Sciences Index
Sociological Abstracts
Television Index
Television News Index and Abstracts (Vanderbilt University Television News Archive)
Topicator
The Wall Street Journal Index
Wilsearch

Newspapers, Magazines, Journals, and Trade Publications

Advertising Age
Billboard
Broadcasting Abroad
Broadcasting and Electronic Media
Cablevision
Columbia Journalism Review
Comment Law Journal
Communication Booknotes

Communication Research Trends
Critical Studies in Mass Com-
  munication
Daily Variety
Electronic Media
Federal Communications Law
  Journal
Feedback
Hollywood Reporter
Journal of Advertising
Journal of Advertising Research
Journal of Broadcasting & Elec-
  tronic Media
Journal of Communication
Journal of Film and Video
Journal of Media Economics
Journal of Popular Culture

Journalism Quarterly
Los Angeles Times
Mass Communication Review
Media and Values
Media, Culture and Society
Media Law Reporter
New York Times
Public Opinion Quarterly
Satellite Week
SMPTE Journal (technical)
Television Digest
Television Quarterly
Television/Radio Age
TV Guide
Variety
Wall St. Journal
Washington Post

Libraries and Museums

Communications Library
University of Illinois
122 Gregory Hall
810 S. Wright Street
Urbana, IL 61801

George Washington University
Gelman Library
Telecommunications Information
  Center
Washington, DC 20052

The Museum of Broadcast Communications
Michigan Avenue at Washington
  Street
Chicago, IL 60606
(Collection of television tapes and
  memorabilia, including vintage
  television sets, and tapes of
  1960 Nixon/Kennedy debate,
  the ABC Wide World of Sports
  collection, and more)

The Museum of Television and
  Radio

25 West 52nd Street
New York, NY 10019
(Collection of over 25,000 television programs and commercials
  on tape, and television scripts
  on microfiche)

The National Museum of Communications
6305 N. O'Connor, Ste. 123
Irving, TX 75039
mailing address: 2001 Plymouth
  Rock, Richardson, TX 75081
(Collection includes replica of a
  1960's television studio, an early
  color television camera, and an
  archive of vintage television
  programs.)

University of Pennsylvania
Annenberg School for Com-
  munications Television Script
  Archive
3620 Walnut Street
Philadelphia, PA 19104

(Approximately 2,500 prime time television scripts)

Vanderbilt University Television News Archives

Vanderbilt University Library
Nashville, TN 37203
(ABC, CBS, and NBC news programs and special events)

Professional Organizations

Academy for Television Arts and Sciences
5220 Lankershim Blvd.
North Hollywood, CA 91601
(818) 754-2800

American Federation of Television and Radio Artists
260 Madison Avenue
New York, NY 10016
(212) 532-0800

Association of Americas Public Television Stations
1350 Connecticut Avenue, N.W.
Washington, DC 20036
(202) 887-1700

Association of Independent Television Stations
1320 19th Street, Suite 300
Washington, DC 20036
(202) 887-1970

Association of Independent Video and Filmmakers, Inc.
625 Broadway
New York, NY 10012
(212) 473-3400

Cable Television Information Center
1700 Shaker Church Road, N.W.
Olympia, WA 98502
(206) 866-2080

Corporation for Public Broadcasting
901 E Street, N.W.
Washington, DC 20004
(202) 879-9600

Directors Guild of America
7920 Sunset Blvd.
Hollywood, CA 90046
(310) 656-1220

Electronic Industries Association
2001 Pennsylvania Avenue, N.W.
Washington, DC 20006
(202) 457-4900

Federal Communications Commission
1919 M Street, N.W.
Washington, DC 20554
(202) 632-7000

National Association of Broadcasters (and Broadcast Education Association)
1771 N Street, N.W.
Washington, DC 20036
(202) 429-5300

National Cable Television Association
1724 Massachusetts Avenue, N.W.
Washington, DC 20036
(202) 775-3550

Society of Motion Picture and Television Engineers
595 Hartsdale Avenue
White Plains, NY 10607
(914) 761-1100

Television Bureau of Advertising
477 Madison Avenue, 10th Floor
New York, NY 10022
(212) 486-1111

United Nations Media Division
New York, NY 10017
(212) 963-6945

Women in Communications, Inc.
P.O. Box 14760
Arlington, VA 22201
(703) 528-4200

Writers Guild of America, East
555 West 57th Street
New York, NY 10019
(212) 245-6180

Writers Guild of America, West
8955 Beverly Blvd.
West Hollywood, CA 90048
(310) 550-1000

Publishers of Television-Related Books

Ablex Publishing Corporation
355 Chestnut Street
Norwood, NJ 07648

Addison-Wesley Publishing
One Jacob Way
Reading, MA 01867
(914) 993-5000

Allyn & Bacon
160 Gould Street
Needham Heights, MA 02194
(800) 852-8024

Artech House
685 Canton Street
Norwood, MA 02062

Basic Books
10 E. 53rd Street
New York, NY 10022

Cambridge University Press
40 West 20th Street
New York, NY 10011
(212) 924-3900

Carol Publishing Group
(Citadel Press, Birch Lane Press,
   Lyle Stuart)
120 Enterprise Avenue
Secaucus, NJ 07094
(201) 866-0490

Columbia University Press
136 South Broadway
Irvington, NY 10533

Doubleday
666 Fifth Avenue
New York, NY 10103
(212) 765-6500

Focal Press
80 Montvale Avenue
Stoneham, MA 02180

The Free Press
866 Third Avenue
New York, NY 10022
(212) 702-5607

Gale Research (Visible Ink Press)
835 Penobscot Building
Detroit, MI 48226
(313) 961-2242

Garland Publishing Co., Inc.
717 Fifth Avenue
New York, NY 10022
Fax (212) 308-9399

Greenwood Publishing
88 Post Road West
P.O. Box 5007
Westport, CT 06881
(203) 226-3571

Harvard University Press
79 Garden Street
Cambridge, MA 02138
(617) 495-2606

Indiana University Press
601 Morton Street
Bloomington, IN 47404
Fax (812) 855-7931

Iowa State University Press
2121 S. State Avenue
Ames, IA 50010
(515) 292-0140

Knowledge Industry Publications
701 Westchester Avenue
White Plains, NY 10604
(914) 328-9157

Lexington Books
125 Spring Street
Lexington, MA 02173
(800) 235-3565

Libraries Unlimited
P.O. Box 6633
Englewood, CO 80155
(800) 237-6124

Longman Publishing
10 Bank Street
White Plains, NY 10601
(914) 993-5000

McFarland & Company, Inc.,
    Publishers
Box 611
Jefferson, NC 28640
(910) 246-4460

McGraw-Hill
1221 Avenue of the Americas
New York, NY 10020
(800) 338-3987

Macmillan Publishing
866 3rd Avenue
New York, NY 10022
(800) 428-3750

Mayfield Publishing
1240 Villa Street
Mountain View, CA 94041
(415) 960-3222

MIT Press
55 Hayward Street
Cambridge, MA 02142
Fax (617) 253-1709

Morrow, William
1350 Avenue of the Americas
New York, NY 10019
(212) 261-6709

Nelson-Hall Publishers
111 N. Canal Street
Chicago, IL 60606
(312) 930-9446

Northwestern University Press
625 Colfax Street
Evanston, IL 60201
(708) 491-5313

NTC Publishing Group
4255 W. Touhy Avenue
Lincolnwood, IL 60646
(800) 323-4900

Oryx Press
4041 N. Central Indian School
    Road
Phoenix, AZ 85012

Oxford University Press
2001 Evans Road
Cary, NC 27513

Penguin USA Publishers
375 Hudson Street
New York, NY 10014
(212) 366-2373

Plenum Press
233 Spring Street
New York, NY 10013
(212) 620-8000

Praeger Publishers
88 Post Road West
Westport, CT 06881
(203) 226-3571

Prentice-Hall
Route 9 West
Englewood Cliffs, NJ 07632
(800) 526-0485

Routledge, Chapman and Hall,
    Inc.
29 West 35th Street
New York, NY 10001
(212) 244-6412

Sage Publications, Inc.
2455 Teller Road
Thousand Oaks, CA 91320-2218
(805) 499-9774

St. Martin's Press
175 Fifth Avenue
New York, NY 10010
(800) 446-8923

Scarecrow Press
52 Liberty Street
Metuchen, NJ 08840
(201) 548-8600

Southern Illinois University Press
Box 3697
Carbondale, IL 62901
(618) 453-6619

TAB Books (McGraw-Hill)
P.O. Box 40
Blue Ridge Summit, PA 17294
(800) 338-3987

Temple University Press
Broad and Oxford Streets
Philadelphia, PA 19122
(215) 787-8787

Transaction Publishers
Rutgers University
New Brunswick, NJ 08903
(908) 932-2280

University of Alabama Press
Box 870380
Tuscaloosa, AL 35487
(205) 348-5180

University of California Press
2120 Berkeley Way
Berkeley, CA 94720
Fax (510) 643-7127

University of Chicago Press
5801 S. Ellis Avenue
Chicago, IL 60637
(312) 702-7748

University of Illinois Press
54 E. Gregory Drive
Champaign, IL 61820

University of Minnesota Press
2037 University Avenue SE
Minneapolis, MN 55414
(612) 624-2516

University of Nebraska Press
901 North 17th Street
Lincoln, NE 68588
(402) 472-3581

University of North Carolina
    Press
P.O. Box 2288
Chapel Hill, NC 27515
(919) 966-3561

University of Pennsylvania Press
418 Service Drive
1300 Blockley Hall
Philadelphia, PA 19104
(215) 898-1673

University of Wisconsin Press
114 N. Murray Street
Madison, WI 53715
(608) 262-8782

Wadsworth Publishing Company
10 Davis Drive
Belmont, CA 94002
(800) 423-0563

Westview Press
5500 Central Avenue
Boulder, CO 80301-2877
(303) 444-3541

INDEX

133